THE WORD THRU TIME

I0461508

CORNELIUS R.

Copyright © 2025 Neale Rawlings.

All rights reserved.

Published under the pen name Cornelius R.

No part of this book may be reproduced, stored in a retrieval system, or transmitted in any form or by any means—electronic, mechanical, photocopying, recording, or otherwise—without prior written permission of the publisher, except for brief quotations in critical articles or reviews.

This is a work of nonfiction.
Scripture quotations, where included, are taken from the King James Version, which is in the public domain.

ISBN (Paperback): 979-8-9937763-2-3

ISBN (Hardcover): 979-8-9937763-3-0

ISBN (eBook): 979-8-9937763-4-7

Cover design: Neale Rawlings

Hardwood Pond Publishing
St. Paul, Minnesota

Printed in the United States of America.

10 9 8 7 6 5 4 3 2 1

Dedication

This book is dedicated to my loving family.

"His faithfulness continues through all generations."

—Psalm 100:5

TABLE OF CONTENTS

TABLE OF CONTENTS (continued)

"The grass withereth, the flower fadeth:
but the word of our God shall stand for ever."

—*Isaiah 40:8*

Chapter 1: The Foundation of the Word

Christ enters time, and time itself changes.

"In the beginning was the Word, and the Word was with God, and the Word was God."
—John 1:1

When the Word stepped into the world, history inhaled. Eternity did not shout its arrival; it slipped quietly into a dusty town in Judea, where shepherds watched the night sky and Roman patrols moved along stone roads. The Creator took on the limits of His creation—not to command from a distance, but to dwell among the ordinary. Time itself would begin to turn around Him.

The world He entered was restless. Rome held the land with iron discipline. Taxes weighed heavily on families who lived from harvest to harvest. Scholars debated in synagogues; zealots quietly spoke of revolt; the poor prayed for deliverance. Into this tension came a carpenter's son with calloused hands and a voice that carried both gentleness and authority. He revealed a Kingdom that did not begin on thrones or in marble halls, but in the human heart.

He spoke in stories drawn from daily life—seeds, lamps, vineyards, fishing nets—so that the unseen could be understood in the language of the simple. When crowds gathered on a hillside overlooking the Sea of Galilee, He spoke words that redefined strength and goodness:

"Blessed are the poor in spirit."

"Blessed are the meek."

"Blessed are the peacemakers."

The Sermon on the Mount was not a new philosophy; it was the announcement of a new world. Where Rome rewarded dominance, He blessed humility. Where the age honored revenge, He commanded love. Where society sorted men by rank, He lifted the unseen and the unimportant. That day, on a quiet hillside, the values of heaven overturned the assumptions of earth.

His teaching ran against the grain of the ancient world. "The last shall be first." "Love your enemies." To His listeners, these words sounded like the unveiling of a world they had always longed for but never believed could exist. To those in authority, they sounded like a quiet revolution. What the empire built through force, He built through invitation. His miracles were restorations, not performances—signs that the world, long bent out of shape, was being straightened.

As His ministry unfolded, a few close followers began to see more of who He truly was. One day, He led Peter, James, and John up a high mountain. There, in a moment no language can fully capture, His face shone like the sun and His garments radiated with unborrowed light. Moses and Elijah appeared beside Him—the Law and the Prophets converging on their fulfillment. A cloud overshadowed them, and a voice said, "This is My beloved Son; listen to Him."

The Transfiguration revealed what the Sermon on the Mount

had implied: the Kingdom He preached was not merely moral but divine, not only interior but eternal. Heaven had touched earth, and earth did not yet know what to do with it.

In Him, the compassion of God took human form. He touched lepers without fear, welcomed children without hesitation, and restored dignity to those society buried in shame. The crowds saw a healer; the leaders saw a threat; His disciples saw glimpses of a Kingdom breaking through the cracks of a weary land.

When He hung between heaven and earth, the Roman world saw the end of a trouble-maker. But heaven saw the turning of the ages. The cross was not defeat but the place where pride met mercy and death met its undoing. The empire believed it was silencing a voice; God was using that silence to begin renewal. Love entered the deepest wound of humanity and rewrote the meaning of sacrifice.

Then dawn broke over an empty tomb, and the world learned that death was not final. The same streets that had watched His ministry now carried whispers of resurrection. Galilean laborers, regular people, journeymen, and widows—those with no standing in the empire—became bearers of the message. The Spirit that hovered at creation now moved through human hearts, binding them into a new kind of community that Rome could neither categorize nor contain.

The Incarnation was not an interruption in the story of the world; it was its center. From this moment forward, every age would be measured by its response to Him—some hearts softening, others hardening, all shaped by the presence of the Word who walked among them.

Christ's coming did more than illuminate a path; it defined reality. In thirty short years, He changed what strength meant, what hope looked like, and what it meant to be human. And the rest of the story—of nations rising and falling, of faith flourishing and fading, of light and darkness contending across centuries—flows from this foundation:

The Word entered time to reclaim it.

Chapter 2: Tribulation and Triumph (33–70 A.D.)

The seed grows in fire.

"But ye shall receive power, after that the Holy Ghost is come upon you: and ye shall be witnesses unto me both in Jerusalem, and in all Judaea, and in Samaria, and unto the uttermost part of the earth." —*Acts 1:8*

When Christ ascended, He left behind no army, no throne, and no wealth—only witnesses. A handful of men and women stood on the Mount of Olives, staring at the sky, charged with an impossible mission: to tell the world that death itself had been defeated. They had no influence, no strategies, and no certainty about the future—only the memory of His words and the promise of His Spirit. From that small circle began the most enduring movement in history. The Word that once walked among them would now work through them.

Ten days later, everything changed. In an upper room in Jerusalem, where fear and hope mingled, a sound like rushing wind filled the house. Tongues of fire rested on each believer, and the timid became bold. The Spirit that hovered over the waters of creation now ignited human hearts. They began to speak in languages they had never learned, proclaiming the works of God to crowds gathered from every corner of the empire. Pentecost reversed Babel: what pride once scattered, grace now united. The nations heard the Gospel in their own language, and the Church took its first breath.

At first, it grew quietly. Families gathered in homes, breaking bread and praying with sincerity that puzzled their neighbors. They sang simple songs, shared their possessions, and cared for the people in need as members of one household. Slaves and scholars sat side by side; merchants and laborers called each other "brother" and "sister." Baptism marked a new identity; the Lord's Supper bound them together. Their faith was not a philosophy—it was a shared life. Rome had never seen a community like this.

But unity of this sort drew attention. A kingdom with no soldiers yet claiming every soul was a threat the empire could not comprehend. The authorities watched with suspicion. In the Temple courts, the apostles preached openly; in the streets, they healed the sick. The Sanhedrin warned them, imprisoned them, and eventually struck at the heart of the movement. Stephen, standing before the council with a face like an angel, became the first to seal his testimony with blood. His martyrdom marked the beginning of open persecution.

Among those approving his death was a young Pharisee named Saul. Zealous for the old order, he made it his mission to crush the new one. He dragged believers from their homes, broke up gatherings, and carried letters authorizing their arrest. But on the road to Damascus, the Light he opposed confronted him. A voice—not accusing but commanding—told him that the Lord he persecuted was, in fact, the Lord he ought to serve. Saul fell blinded, but rose transformed. The persecutor became the preacher. In one conversion, God revealed a pattern that would echo through history: what the enemy meant for destruction became fuel for faith.

Persecution scattered the believers, but each scattering spread the seed farther. Philip preached in Samaria; Peter baptized a Roman centurion; Antioch became a new center of mission. The Church learned that the Gospel was not tied to Jerusalem but destined for the world. As more Gentiles came to faith, the question of belonging reached a crisis. The apostles gathered for the first great council. In Jerusalem, under the leadership of James, they discerned the Spirit's guidance: Gentiles were welcomed without becoming Jews. The Kingdom was larger than culture, older than tradition, and open to all. This decision ensured that Christianity would not become a regional sect but a global faith.

The apostles carried this message across seas and deserts. Peter and Paul reached the heart of the empire itself. Wherever they went, synagogues divided, cities stirred, and hearts awakened. Miracles accompanied their preaching; suffering did as well. They were beaten, imprisoned, and opposed, yet their voices only grew stronger. The Gospel was not contained by walls or ethnicity—it was written for the world.

Meanwhile, tension in Jerusalem tightened like a drawn bow. The city that had rejected its Messiah soon strained under political unrest, false prophets, and revolutionary zeal. Rome marched to restore order, but revolt spread like wildfire. By 70 A.D., the unthinkable had begun. Legions surrounded the city. Famine swept through its streets. The cries of the starving echoed against the Temple walls. When the final breach came, the sanctuary—the heart of worship for a thousand years—fell in smoke and ruin. The stones Jesus said would not remain upon one another were thrown down. With the destruction of the Temple, an age closed. The old covenant had fulfilled its purpose; the new one stood unshaken.

This was the first great cracking of a seal in history. What was earthly and proud collapsed; what was spiritual and eternal endured. God's dwelling no longer stood in stone but lived in His people. The priesthood had become universal, the altar moved into human hearts. The Kingdom survived its first fire because its foundation was not a building but a Person. And just as Jerusalem fell when it tried to silence the Word, Rome would soon follow—every kingdom that resists the Gospel becomes the very soil in which it spreads.

By the time the smoke cleared, the Church had no homeland but heaven and no power but truth. It owned nothing, yet possessed everything. Its Scriptures were being written; its leaders were being martyred; its faith was being refined. The blood of the saints became the ink of testimony. In Rome's prisons, believers sang hymns. In villages and marketplaces, they forgave their accusers. On execution grounds, they died with hope. Courage of this kind confounded the empire, not because it was loud, but because it was steady.

The seed had taken root. In the world's eyes they were outcasts; in heaven's eyes they were founders. Their endurance under persecution revealed the hidden strength of the Kingdom. Tribulation did not destroy the Church—it defined it. Out of ashes came the architecture of belief, built not by decree but by devotion. The faith of the few would become the inheritance of nations.

From this first generation, history learned its rhythm: light born through suffering, truth tested by trial, resurrection following ruin. What began in Jerusalem would outlive the empire that sought to silence it. The early Church lived what the cross had already proven—that in God's design, defeat is never final.

The Church born in suffering became the vessel of His presence.

Chapter 3: The Beast and the Blood (70–200 A.D.)

The empire that tried to crush the Word reveals its own nature.

"Babylon the great is fallen"
—Revelation 18:2

After the fall of Jerusalem in 70 A.D., the center of the Christian story moved into the heart of the empire that once crucified its Lord. The Church had no Temple, no homeland, and no political shield—only the presence of Christ and the memory of His promise. Rome, triumphant after crushing Judea, believed it had silenced a troublesome sect. But in truth, the scattering of believers had carried the seed of the Kingdom far beyond the city's ruins. What looked like defeat was the beginning of an age where the contrast between the Word and the world would be revealed in fire.

Rome entered these years at the height of its power. The Flavian emperors—Vespasian, Titus, and Domitian—displayed the wealth of the empire with pride. Taxes and war spoils funded colossal projects. The Colosseum, begun in the early 70s using Jewish slave labor, rose as a monument to imperial mastery. It became Rome's beating heart: a place where crowds gathered to cheer as men battled beasts and prisoners died for spectacle. Blood became entertainment, and cruelty turned into civic ceremony. The same empire that boasted of peace built an arena where death was sport. Its grandeur concealed a spiritual void.

Across the city stood the Pantheon, a masterpiece of Roman engineering, dedicated to the gods of the empire. Its open dome symbolized the heavens; its altars honored every deity Rome believed could grant success. It was the architecture of religious tolerance—so long as every worship eventually bowed to Caesar. This was the soul of the empire: many gods welcomed, one Lord forbidden. To confess Jesus as *Kyrios*— Lord—was to deny the emperor's divinity. It was not considered a spiritual claim but an act of treason.

Christians therefore gathered in houses, workshops, fields, and at times in catacombs carved beneath the city. They shared quietly and prayed in the dark, where the empire's ears could not reach. Their faith did not fade under pressure; it deepened. Charity became their signature. Outcasts were fed, orphans protected, slaves welcomed as equals. A new kind of community was forming—one defined not by power but by love. This was the first crack in the Beast: the empire commanded fear; the Church practiced compassion.

Yet the empire struck back. Nero's brutality had set a precedent, and though persecution did not rage continuously, it returned like waves. Under Domitian, emperor worship became compulsory. Those who refused faced exile, imprisonment, or death. Among them was the apostle John, exiled to the rocky island of Patmos. There, far from the marble halls of Rome, he received visions that unveiled the spiritual reality behind the empire's glittering façade.

Revelation was not written to confuse but to console. It revealed that the powers of the world—no matter how strong —were temporary, and that behind Rome's splendor lurked a Beast doomed to fall. The imagery of seals, trumpets, and judgments showed that history itself belonged to the Lamb. To a Church suffering beneath imperial pressure, John's visions were assurance that God was not silent, and that the empire's arrogance would one day meet divine justice.

When Trajan became emperor (98–117 A.D.), persecution grew more formal. Pliny the Younger, a provincial governor, wrote to him asking how to handle Christians. His letter gives a vivid glimpse of early worship: believers gathered at dawn, sang "to Christ as to a god," bound themselves by oath to honesty, and shared a common meal. Pliny found no crimes in them except their refusal to worship Rome's gods. Trajan's reply became imperial policy: Christians were not to be hunted, but if accused and refusing to recant, they were to be punished—even executed. The empire feared their loyalty to a higher King.

As the second century unfolded, the empire's brilliance reached its height. Under Hadrian and Antoninus Pius, peace and stability flourished. Roads stretched across continents; law and order touched distant provinces. But beneath the marble lay cracks. Philosophers sensed the emptiness of pagan religion. Gladiatorial games, once thrilling, began to expose Rome's appetite for violence. And quietly, steadily, Christians grew in number and reputation. Their lives of purity and charity unsettled a culture accustomed to indulgence.

In this era arose voices like Justin Martyr, who defended the faith with voice and reason. He argued that the Logos—the Word—had entered the world, and that the teachings of Christ completed what philosophers had sought in fragments. His writings gave Christianity intellectual credibility in a world hungry for truth. Yet he, too, died a martyr. The empire admired virtue but feared conviction.

Then came the Antonine plague (c. 165–180 A.D.), carried back from the eastern campaigns. It ravaged cities and armies alike, killing millions. Temples filled with smoke; priests begged the gods for relief. But no answer came. Panic spread as bodies lined the streets. Pagan families abandoned the sick for fear of infection. Physicians fled. Only the Christians stayed. They nursed the dying, fed the weak, and buried the forgotten. Many believers died from the compassion they offered, yet their sacrifice transformed public perception. Rome saw that the people it once despised were its truest caretakers.

Meanwhile, the empire's stability began to crumble. Marcus Aurelius, the philosopher-emperor, sought to revive Roman virtue, yet he viewed Christians as obstinate enemies of the old order. Under his reign, local persecutions flared. In Lyon and Smyrna, believers suffered torture and execution. Among them was Polycarp, a bishop in his 80s, who, when ordered to curse Christ, replied simply, "Eighty and six years have I served Him, and He has done me no wrong." His calm martyrdom revealed the empire's powerlessness before a single faithful soul.

By the late second century, decay crept further into Rome's heart. Commodus turned the throne into a spectacle. Corruption spread through the Senate and army. Generals rose and fell by assassination. The empire that once boasted of eternal strength began to tremble beneath its own weight. Yet in homes and villages, believers continued to pray, care, and persevere. Their endurance revealed another crack in the Beast: an empire built on fear cannot comprehend a people who do not fear death.

By 200 A.D., Rome still stood—its temples gleaming, its legions marching—but its soul had begun to crumble. Its public virtue was hollow, its gods silent, its leaders unstable. And beneath the marble, a new world was rising. The Church, once hidden in houses and caves, had become the quiet conscience of civilization. It carried no swords, demanded no tribute, and claimed no land, yet it had something the empire could not manufacture—hope.

The Beast had roared for over a century, but its voice began to waver. The first seal had cracked. What was proud began to falter; what was humble began to rise. And in the shadows of Rome's grandeur, the Word endured, preparing for the moment when the empire that once nailed Christ to a cross would feel the weight of its own unraveling.

The empire's cruelty revealed its nature; the Church's endurance revealed its truth.

16

Chapter 4: The Empire in Crisis (200–312 A.D.)

The old world burns while a new world takes root.

"He that shall endure unto the end, the same shall be saved." —
Matthew 24:13

After the first century of persecution and quiet growth, the Church entered a new and darker age. Rome still called itself eternal, but its foundations had begun to shake. The marble temples remained, the legions marched, and the Senate still gathered beneath painted ceilings—but beneath the surface, the empire's soul was unraveling. The second and third centuries would reveal an ancient truth: when nations exalt themselves, they collapse under their own weight. And when the world grows weary, the Kingdom of God grows strong.

By the late second century, Rome's moral exhaustion had become visible. Commodus, son of Marcus Aurelius, traded virtue for spectacle, turning the throne into a stage. Bribery flourished in the Senate, assassinations plagued the palace, and legions sold their loyalty to the highest bidder. What had once been a disciplined empire became a marketplace of power. Pagan religion, once the heart of Rome's identity, grew hollow. Priests offered sacrifice without conviction; philosophers admitted the gods had grown silent.

Yet in the shadows of decline, the Church continued to rise. Christians were known for honesty in business, purity in conduct, and charity toward the poor. Pagan writers, though hostile to their faith, grudgingly admired their character. While Rome pursued pleasure, the believers pursued holiness. While the empire clung to wealth, they practiced generosity. In a decaying world, the Church became the quiet conscience of civilization.

Then the empire entered its darkest century.

The Fifty Years of Chaos (200–250 A.D.)

From 235 to 284 A.D., Rome suffered what history calls the Crisis of the Third Century—yet even that phrase seems too gentle for the chaos that erupted. In fifty years, more than twenty emperors rose and fell, most of them murdered by their own soldiers. Provinces broke away to form rival empires. Barbarians crossed frontiers with growing confidence. Inflation soared; the economy collapsed; famine stalked entire regions. A world that once boasted stability now tasted the fragility of its own greatness.

Amid these crises, the Church grew deeper roots. Leaders emerged who shaped doctrine and unity. Bishops guided scattered communities; elders shepherded flocks in cities and villages. Letters circulated, gospels were copied, and the contours of the canon began to take shape. The faith that had lived in house-churches now developed structure—not as an institution of power, but as a body learning to survive.

Then came another plague.

The Antonine plague had shaken the empire a generation earlier, but now the Cyprian plague swept across the Mediterranean like a shadow. From Egypt to Gaul, entire towns emptied. Bodies lay abandoned in the streets; families fled from their own sick. Pagan priests hid behind temple doors. Fear ruled every province.

Only the Christians stayed.

They nursed the dying, fed the weak, comforted the abandoned, and buried the forgotten. Many believers died from the compassion they offered, but their sacrifice transformed public perception. Bishop Cyprian of Carthage taught that suffering did not destroy faith—it refined it. He urged his flock to love the dying even at the cost of their own lives. In an age of terror, the Church embodied a courage the empire could not manufacture.

The plague exposed Rome's wounds and revealed the Church's strength. The empire's gods had no answer; its philosophers had no comfort. But Christians offered hope— not by escaping suffering, but by entering it. This was another crack in the Beast.

Rome's leaders believed the empire's crises stemmed from neglected gods. To them, the solution was a return to old rituals. Emperor Decius sought to restore Rome's glory through religious unity. For the first time in imperial history, every citizen was required to offer incense to the Roman gods and receive a certificate proving loyalty.

Christians could not comply.

For many, the cost was brutal. Those who refused were imprisoned, tortured, or killed. Others, overwhelmed by fear, complied and later sought forgiveness. The Church was torn: should those who had lapsed be restored? Local churches agonized, some locking the doors, others opening them in mercy. This crisis revealed both the weakness and strength of early believers: they were human enough to stumble, but Christlike enough to forgive.

Decius's reign was short; he died in battle, and the persecution eased. But the empire had tasted the idea of enforced worship —and it would return to it with greater fury.

Under Emperor Valerian, persecution sharpened. Instead of targeting all Christians, Rome went after their leaders. Bishops, presbyters, and deacons were arrested. Church property was confiscated. Worship was driven underground once more.

But even this strategy backfired. When shepherds were killed, new leaders rose in their place. When buildings were seized, worship returned to houses. When Rome tried to silence voices, it amplified them. The Church learned to live without structural comforts. Faith became simpler, purer, and harder to break.

Then, unexpectedly, the pressure lifted. Valerian was captured in battle by Persian forces—a humiliation the empire never forgot—and his son Gallienus issued the first imperial edict of toleration. For the first time in decades, Christians breathed in peace. But Rome still stood on fragile ground.

As the empire sought to restore its strength, a new religious vision emerged. Emperor Aurelian attempted to unify Rome under the worship of *Sol Invictus*—the Unconquered Sun. Temples rose; festivals expanded; the empire clung desperately to the idea that divine favor could be regained through ritual. Christianity remained officially tolerated, but suspicion simmered. Rome was trying to save itself by summoning gods who no longer answered.

Then came Diocletian.

He reorganized the empire into the Tetrarchy, revived discipline in the legions, and attempted to rebuild Rome's identity through religious conformity. Pagan sacrifice became a political duty. Unity was enforced through worship. And to Diocletian, the Christians were a threat—not because they were powerful, but because they bowed to a King Rome could not command.

In 303 A.D., he launched what history calls the **Great Persecution**—the most violent and systematic assault the Church had ever faced. Churches were burned; Scriptures destroyed; clergy imprisoned; Christian rights revoked. Many believers were executed for refusing to sacrifice to the gods. It was the empire's attempt to purge the Kingdom from its midst.

But the Church had endured too much to break.

Where Scriptures were burned, believers recited them from memory. Where churches were destroyed, homes became sanctuaries again. Where bishops were imprisoned, laypeople led. The persecution did not extinguish the Church—it purified it. The empire struck with its full strength, yet its blows fell on a faith that had already learned to suffer well.

Even pagan observers noted the paradox: the more Rome attacked, the stronger the Christians became.

Diocletian retired in 305, the first emperor to voluntarily leave the throne. But the Tetrarchy he crafted fell apart instantly. Civil wars erupted as rivals fought for control. Four emperors became six, then eight. The empire entered a spiritual exhaustion deeper than any plague.

And in the midst of the chaos, Christians continued to pray, serve, and endure. They had become a people the empire could neither defeat nor ignore. Rome's power was still visible, but its confidence had vanished. The Beast was bleeding out.

By 312 A.D., a young general named Constantine rose in the West, moving toward a confrontation that would reshape the world. But that moment belongs to the next chapter. For now, the story ends with an empire weary from its own fury and a Church still standing—wounded, refined, unshaken.

Rome had tried everything—laws, prisons, swords, fire, and fear. But the Kingdom it opposed could not be killed. It had survived plagues, tyrants, chaos, and persecution because it was built on the Word.

The empire's collapse prepared the way for its conversion. The fire that tried to destroy the Church became the fire that refined it.

Chapter 5: The Turning of the Age (300–600 A.D.)

Rome bows, Christendom rises.

"By this sign, conquer."
—Vision of Constantine, A.D. 312

The Beast had spent its fury. For three centuries Rome had hunted the followers of the Word, yet the Church endured. What persecution could not kill, corruption could not weaken, and fear could not silence began now to stand in the open. The empire that once claimed eternity trembled beneath famine, civil war, and spiritual despair. Its legions fought one another more than foreign foes. Its temples filled with smoke but not with hope. The gods were silent; the world was weary. Into this exhaustion stepped a soldier named Constantine.

In the struggle for imperial power, he marched toward a decisive battle at the Milvian Bridge. On the eve of conflict, as ancient sources recall, he looked to the sky and saw a sign —a cross of light above the sun, with the words In hoc signo vinces: "By this sign, conquer." Whether seen by the eye or the conscience, the vision marked him. Constantine ordered his troops to paint the Christ-sign on their shields. The next day, he prevailed. The imperial world shifted.

In A.D. 313, the Edict of Milan ended centuries of persecution. Prisons opened; bishops emerged from hiding; families reclaimed their martyrs' bodies; churches rose where torture chambers had stood. For the first time since Pentecost, the Gospel breathed freely in the open air. Constantine himself was not a theologian, nor was his conversion perfect or complete in a moment. But he knew one thing clearly: the God who had carried slaves, fishermen, and exiles had carried him as well. And so the axis of history turned.

His mother Helena journeyed to the Holy Land, establishing churches at the sites of Christ's passion and resurrection. Shrines replaced shrines; the empire that once tried to erase the memory of Jesus now preserved it in stone. Yet this new freedom brought new tests. A persecuted Church had learned humility, patience, and courage. A favored Church now had to learn discernment. Influence can corrupt as easily as violence can wound.

The fourth century opened with the Church stepping into stewardship. Temples became churches. Pagan festivals were given Christian meaning. But faith spread too swiftly for purity to keep pace. Alongside genuine devotion came ambition; alongside worship came politics. The empire baptized itself in haste, and not all the water was clean. Even so, truth flowed beneath the surface.

A crisis soon revealed the need for clarity. Arius, a presbyter from Alexandria, taught that Christ was exalted above creation but not eternal—"There was a time when the Son was not." Churches divided; bishops argued; whole cities rioted. The question was no mere debate of scholars; it concerned the very identity of the Word made flesh.

In A.D. 325, Constantine summoned bishops from across the known world to the Council of Nicaea. Old men who had lost eyes or limbs in persecution now gathered beside young leaders raised in peace. Their voices echoed across the hall as they affirmed what the Church had always known: the Son is not a creation but the eternal Word, "begotten, not made, being of one substance with the Father." A people's proclamation became a universal creed. The faith that once hid in catacombs now shaped the conscience of emperors.

As the empire weakened, the Church strengthened. The Word moved into new landscapes—frontiers the legions had lost. Missionaries carried the Gospel beyond imperial borders, not with swords but with story, song, and sacrifice. Ulfilas translated Scripture for the Goths; Martin of Tours preached in the fields of Gaul; Patrick traveled among the Irish, lighting a fire that would one day illuminate Europe.

While missionaries moved outward, another movement grew inward. In Egypt, a young man named Antony heard the Gospel's call and withdrew into the desert. His life of prayer and solitude attracted others. Soon the deserts of Egypt and Syria flourished with spiritual communities—men and women who chose poverty over privilege and silence over applause. Pachomius organized communal monastic life; Basil the Great would later refine it. Athanasius, exiled from his own see, wrote the Life of Antony, and the ideals of monastic discipline spread westward like a fresh wind. When the empire fractured, these communities became wells of stability, preserving Scripture, labor, and learning while cities burned.

In A.D. 382, another foundation was laid: Jerome began translating the Scriptures into Latin. His work, the Vulgate, gave the Western world a unified Bible. As Rome declined, the Word became its anchor.

The empire's fall came slowly, not in a single blow. In A.D. 410, the Visigoths stormed the Eternal City. For eight centuries Rome had stood unconquered; now its gates fell. Pagan voices blamed the Christians, claiming the old gods had abandoned Rome because new faith had replaced them. But in North Africa, a bishop named Augustine offered a deeper vision. In The City of God, he argued that no earthly empire can claim eternity. The City of Man rises and falls; the City of God endures forever. Rome's collapse was not the collapse of truth—it was the unveiling of a world built on pride.

The fifth century unfolded with sorrow and possibility. Western Rome dissolved into fragments. Kings ruled where emperors once strode. Yet amid the ruin, the Church became the thread that kept society from tearing apart. Bishops negotiated peace, ransomed captives, protected the poor, and preserved learning. Monasteries turned wilderness into cultivated land. Songs of prayer echoed where armies once camped. A new civilization—still fragile, still flawed—took root.

By the sixth century, this transformation was visible across the landscape. Cathedrals rose where pagan temples had crumbled. Law bent slowly toward mercy. Slaves found dignity, widows protection, strangers hospitality. The world had not become perfect—far from it—but the direction of history had changed. Violence no longer ruled unchecked; cruelty no longer defined public life; children, once discarded without thought, were now seen as gifts of God. Light had entered the framework of culture itself.

In A.D. 609, a final symbol marked the end of an age. The Pantheon—Rome's great temple to every god—was consecrated as a church dedicated to the one true God. Its oculus, once open to Jupiter and Mars, now opened to heaven alone. Marble built for idols now echoed with psalms. What Rome had constructed for pride became a monument to grace. History turned a page.

The age of Caesars had ended; the age of Christendom had begun. Satan's chains, once loosened in the violence of pagan empire, were drawn tight. The unrestrained cruelty of the ancient world gave way to the order of grace. There were still weeds among the wheat, and shadows still clung to the morning, but a new light governed the horizon. The Church no longer hid—it built. It no longer endured alone—it shaped.

By the close of A.D. 600, the world was not the same world that crucified Christ or hunted His followers. It bore instead the imprint of the One who said, "Behold, I make all things new." From ashes to order, from empire to Kingdom, a new chapter had begun.

From ashes to order, the reign begins.

Chapter 6: The Quiet Kingdom (600–1100 A.D.)

Light rebuilds what war destroyed.

"Except the Lord build the house, they labor in vain."
—Psalm 127:1

When Rome fell, the world did not shatter—it shifted. The marble roads cracked, the legions scattered, and the old rhythms of empire dissolved into silence. But in that silence, something new began. What the Caesars had forged with iron, the Church now shaped with patience. The age of conquest ended; the age of cultivation began. Across the scarred landscape of Europe, the Gospel settled into the soil. Its work was slow, quiet, persistent—more like dawn than lightning.

The first builders of this new world were not kings but monks.

I. The Monastic Dawn

In the ruins of former provinces, men and women withdrew into wilderness seeking God. They fled not from life, but toward order—carrying with them Scripture, prayer, and a rhythm of work. On wind-swept coasts and in deep forests, monasteries rose like embers glowing in ash. Benedict of

Nursia had written a simple rule a century earlier—*ora et labora*, pray and work—and his vision took root across Europe.

Within stone walls lit by flickering candles, scribes bent over parchment. They copied Scripture line by line, stroke by careful stroke. In those scriptoria, the memory of the world was preserved. Not only Bibles, but histories, poems, medical texts, and mathematics survived because hands shaped by prayer shaped ink as well. Civilization did not die; it hid in monasteries until it could breathe again.

Life in these communities flowed like a true liturgy: sunrise prayer, morning labor, noon reading, evening reflection. The bell tower became the clock of Europe, calling towns and fields into a rhythm of devotion. Time itself was baptized. Where Rome had measured life by tax and tribute, the Church measured it by prayer and mercy.

II. The Architecture of Light

As stability grew, stone began to rise toward heaven. Cathedrals replaced pagan temples—not as monuments to power, but as instruments of worship. Their very architecture was a sermon. Thick walls spoke of God's strength; high windows of His grace. When sunlight passed through stained glass, the Scriptures became radiant stories for the illiterate. Every color taught. Every arch pointed upward.

Bells rang across valleys with a sound that carried both command and comfort. They told farmers when to labor and when to rest. They marked feasts and fasts, births and burials, dawns and dusks. In a world once defined by the will of emperors, bells now synchronized the breath of whole regions. Christ's reign sounded like peace and bronze, summoning a village to prayer.

Art and music turned toward heaven. Gregorian chant emerged from monasteries—simple, pure, contemplative. It rose like incense, echoing the stillness of desert prayer. Harmony became a form of devotion; geometry a form of praise. Beauty was not luxury; it was theology made visible. Through art, the weary encountered what words could not yet explain.

III. A New Kind of Power

Across Europe, tribes that had once warred with Rome now listened to the Gospel. Missionaries traveled through forests and over mountains carrying nothing but Scripture and courage. Augustine of Canterbury brought the faith to England; Boniface felled pagan oaks in Germany and planted chapels in their shade; Columbanus and his companions crossed seas to teach Irish kings.

Where empire failed to civilize, the Word succeeded. It taught justice to rulers, mercy to warriors, and dignity to the poor. Kings once defined by conquest now bowed before bishops. The Church did not govern nations—yet it governed the conscience of those who did.

Law bent slowly toward compassion. The sanctity of life, once cheap in the ancient world, became a principle woven into custom. Orphans found protectors; widows advocates;

the sick caregivers. The idea of the hospital, the orphanage, and eventually the university germinated in this soil. The faith that once hid in catacombs now shaped the very concept of human worth.

IV. The Healing of the Land

Monasteries did not only preserve books—they preserved creation. Monks drained swamps, cleared forests, cultivated orchards, and built mills that turned rivers into energy. They understood the land as gift and responsibility. Each act of cultivation was an act of worship—an outward sign of inward order.

From their labor flowed prosperity. Abandoned fields yielded harvests again. Roads reopened. Markets revived. Knowledge spread outward like seed. Civilization healed not through conquest but through care. The world reordered itself around trust rather than fear.

V. Culture Under a Quiet King

The reign of Christ in this era was not political, but cultural— it moved in conscience, education, and compassion. His crown was invisible, yet His influence unmistakable. He ruled through those who prayed, studied, built, forgave, and taught.

This was the period when Satan's chains, loosened in the violence of the pagan age, were drawn tight. The wild cruelty of antiquity was restrained; the destructive idols silenced. It was not a utopia; pride still walked beside devotion, and ambition shadowed every good work. But a new moral imagination had entered the bloodstream of civilization.

People learned to see themselves not as tools of the state or prizes of war, but as souls made in the image of God. That single idea reordered society more deeply than any law could.

VI. Imperfections in the Light

Not all was pure. Wealth accumulated in holy places. Superstition mingled with sincere faith. Some clergy sought influence more than humility. Political rulers at times tried to control the Church, and the Church at times tried to shape politics too strongly. In the heart of every age, wheat and weeds still grow together.

But these shadows never defined the age. The greater truth remained: the Gospel had moved from survival to creation. It no longer hid from the world; it shaped it. Light was not merely resisting darkness—it was organizing the world.

VII. The Quiet Triumph

By the eleventh century, Europe had been transformed. Not by decree, but by devotion. Not by sword, but by Scripture. The scattered tribes of a broken continent had become a tapestry woven by faith. Cathedrals crowned cities; monasteries dotted valleys; learning awakened; hospitality spread. A new civilization—rooted in the Word—stood ready for its next ascent.

The age between 600 and 1100 was not the dramatic era of battles or empires. It was the slow, patient triumph of grace. It was the season when Christ's reign flowed through culture —through bells, books, fields, and families—ordering life from the inside out.

His Kingdom grew not in spectacle, but in silence. Not in power, but in persistence. And though the world remained imperfect, the direction of history had turned decisively toward the light.

Light organizes the world.

Chapter 7: The High Light (1100–1300 A.D.)

When beauty became a form of worship.

"Lift up your hearts."
—The Sursum Corda

By the eleventh century, Europe had been rebuilt enough to breathe—slowly at first, then deeply. The seeds planted by monks in the quiet centuries after Rome's fall now pushed upward. The land was cultivated, the faith was rooted, and the rhythm of prayer had shaped whole generations. What emerged next was not merely recovery but radiance. The continent awoke to a new possibility: that all of life—art, law, learning, music, craftsmanship—could be shaped as an offering to Christ.

This era did not erupt with drama; it unfolded with harmony. The world felt newly coherent. The Gospel had settled into the bones of civilization, and now civilization responded with beauty. The High Middle Ages became the moment when the Christian imagination reached its height. Everything turned toward God—not by force, but by desire.

I. The Ascent of Stone

The first sign of this flowering appeared in architecture. In villages and cities across Europe, builders dreamed of churches that did not simply house worship but embodied it. Romanesque forms gave way to something new—an architecture of ascent. Pointed arches lifted the eye upward; ribbed vaults carried weight with grace; flying buttresses freed walls for windows of light.

These were not technical innovations alone—they were theological statements in stone. The builders sought to mirror the order of heaven. Geometry reflected divine harmony; proportion expressed the balance of creation. Every line invited contemplation. Every pillar symbolized the apostles. Every window taught the Scriptures.

But medieval builders understood something deeper still: **sound was part of healing,** and God's world could be tuned.

The great cathedrals were designed as instruments. Their vaults captured resonance; their stones carried vibration. Chants rose, lingered, and returned softened by the air itself. Frequencies intertwined with light, shaping the experience of prayer. The wounded and weary entered these spaces not only to hear truth but to be *bathed* in it—through color, sound, and stillness. The very architecture participated in Christ's reign, becoming a vessel of peace.

When sunlight passed through stained glass, the Gospel became illumination. When choirs sang in perfect intervals, theology became harmony. The cathedral was not only a house of worship; it was a sacrament of culture. It taught through beauty, healed through resonance, and lifted humanity toward contemplation.

II. The Rise of the University

As cathedrals rose, so did learning. The twelfth and thirteenth centuries birthed something unprecedented: the university. In Paris, Bologna, Oxford, and later Cologne and Padua, schools gathered around cathedrals and monasteries until they became centers of study unlike any the world had seen.

Students came from every land, walking miles to sit on benches in drafty halls, eager to understand the order they saw in nature and Scripture. Teachers developed a new method—**scholasticism**—dedicated to seeking harmony between faith and reason. Questions were not feared; they were welcomed. Truth could stand examination precisely because truth was unified.

Anselm prayed that he might "believe in order to understand." Abelard argued that understanding deepened belief. Aquinas brought them together, showing that reason was not the enemy of faith but its servant. In his great *Summa*, he arranged the world like a cathedral of thought— each argument a rib supporting a greater structure, each conclusion a window letting in clearer light.

The university was Christendom's intellectual cathedral. It trained theologians, lawyers, physicians, poets, and philosophers. It assumed the unity of truth because it assumed the unity of God. Learning was not merely practical; it was sacred.

Knowledge became a way to love God with the mind.

III. The Age of Reforming Orders

If the Benedictines had built stability, the new orders brought movement. The twelfth and thirteenth centuries saw the rise of men and women who carried the Gospel into streets, marketplaces, and courts. Francis of Assisi walked barefoot among the poor, preaching simplicity, humility, and joy. His love for creation reminded the world that the God who ordered the stars also adorned the lilies of the field.

Dominic founded an order devoted to preaching truth with clarity and compassion. His followers studied rigorously so that their words could heal error rather than merely defeat it. Together, the Franciscan and Dominican movements renewed cities, corrected excesses, and reminded rulers that faith must be lived, not merely professed.

Their presence crowned the era: one order teaching the world to love God with the heart, the other teaching it to love Him with the mind. Both were responses to Christ's reign, carried into the bustling centers of medieval life.

IV. A Civilization in Harmony

By the mid-thirteenth century, Europe pulsed with new coherence. Art flourished in manuscripts gilded with gold and painted with scenes from Scripture. Music advanced through polyphony—lines of melody woven like voices in prayer. Law reflected Christian ethics, slowly bending toward justice, restraint, and the dignity of every soul.

Guilds governed trade with fairness, protecting workers, regulating quality, and giving charity to those in need.

Pilgrimages connected distant lands, weaving a web of shared devotion. Cities grew but retained a sense of sacred order. Every square had a church; every market a cross; every calendar a cycle of feasts and fasts.

This was not the triumph of one nation or ruler. It was the convergence of countless acts of faith: builders carving stone, scribes illuminating texts, farmers resting on holy days, choirs practicing with devotion, judges ruling with conscience, families praying at night. It was the quiet reign of Christ reaching its visible height.

The ancient world measured greatness by conquest. Medieval Christendom measured greatness by alignment—how fully life could reflect the beauty, truth, and order of God.

V. Shadows Beneath the Heights

Even in this radiant age, imperfections remained. Pride crept into scholarship; ambition touched the Church; kings sometimes sought to control the very faith that disciplined them. Wars flared at the edges of Christendom, and some holy causes became entangled with human motives. Not every cathedral was built with pure hands; not every dispute was settled with grace.

But these shadows did not overturn the greater light. They reminded the world that human institutions, even when shaped by the Gospel, remain human. Wheat and weeds still grew together, yet the fields of Europe glowed with unprecedented beauty.

VI. The High Light Reaches Its Zenith

By 1300, Christendom stood as the most ordered, educated, and creative civilization the world had ever seen. Not perfect —never perfect—but profoundly shaped by the Word. The Gospel had moved from survival to culture, from culture to harmony. Its influence was visible in every discipline, every craft, every cathedral spire piercing the sky.

Everything in this age was designed—consciously, reverently —to be worthy of Christ:

- geometry to reflect His order

- music to echo His peace

- law to express His justice

- charity to embody His compassion

- learning to seek His truth

- art to reveal His beauty

The era was not a utopia. But it was a testimony.

A testimony that when Christ's reign moves through hearts and conscience rather than coercion. And through beauty rather than power—the world flourishes.

Christ ruled this age with harmony.

Not with decrees, but with desire.

Not with domination, but with light.

Society reaches its height.

Chapter 8: The Breaking Twilight (1300–1500 A.D.)

When harmony lingers even as the frame begins to crack.

"Although the fig tree shall not blossom… yet I will rejoice in the LORD."
— Habakkuk 3:17–18

By the dawn of the fourteenth century, Christendom stood at its height. Cathedrals crowned cities, choirs wove worship into the very air, and the rhythm of Christian life shaped all of Europe. Yet beneath this brilliance, strains began to emerge— subtle at first, then unmistakable. The great house of faith was still standing, still beautiful, still full of devotion, but small fractures ran through the beams. Twilight approached not as sudden darkness, but as fading light.

The age to come would not destroy the world built by the Gospel, but it would test it. And in those tests, the quiet splendor of Christian culture would shine with unexpected intensity.

The unity that had defined the High Middle Ages began to loosen. Kings grew more powerful and more ambitious, claiming authority once reserved for the Church. The papacy, long a moral anchor, became entangled in politics. Wealth collected in certain sees; rivalries brewed among nations; clerical offices were sometimes granted more for influence than devotion.

None of this overturned the essential goodness of the age, but it created fissures—small lines of tension that would widen over time. The people remained faithful, the monasteries remained steady, the liturgy remained the heartbeat of Europe. Yet the institutional harmony of Christendom was no longer seamless.

The world was changing, and the Church, though still radiant, felt the strain.

Then came the blow that reshaped everything.
In 1347, ships arrived in European harbors carrying a pestilence unseen in living memory. The plague spread with a speed that defied understanding. Towns emptied; cities fell silent; processions of the dying replaced markets. It is estimated that a third, perhaps half of Europe perished.

The horror was real, but so was the devotion. Priests died anointing the sick. Monks tended the dying until they themselves succumbed. Mothers buried children; children buried parents; communities buried entire generations. Fear mingled with faith. Sorrow deepened prayer. Questions rose —Why this suffering? Where is God in such silence?—yet even these questions were shaped by belief.

The plague did not break Christendom's faith, but it bruised its spirit. When the Black Death passed, the world it left behind was humbler, more fragile, more aware of its mortality. The memory of death did not extinguish light, but it softened it. Twilight entered the soul of Europe.

As if grief were not enough, a wound of another kind followed.

In 1309, the papacy relocated to Avignon, a move seen by many as submission to political powers. For nearly seventy years, the popes ruled from a palace far from Rome. Meanwhile, corruption crept into administration, and voices called for reform.

Then came the Great Western Schism (1378–1417). Two men claimed to be pope—then three. Ordinary Christians, who had looked to the papacy as the visible sign of unity, found themselves confused and disheartened. Bishops were divided; kings took sides; councils struggled to heal the breach.

Yet even in this turmoil, the deeper reality held:
The faith itself did not fracture.
The Gospel did not diminish.
The liturgy did not falter.
The sacraments continued.
The people remained faithful.

The house shook, but the foundation stood.

And here lies one of the great paradoxes of history:
Just as political and institutional unity strained, the creativity of Christendom reached new brilliance.

Far from dimming, the artistic imagination of the age glowed with fresh intensity.

1. The International Gothic Style

Painters and sculptors created works of extraordinary grace:

- illuminated manuscripts shimmering with gold

- altarpieces glowing with deep blues and reds

- elegant figures in devotional scenes

- delicate lines and luminous faces

The **Books of Hours**, prayer books for laypeople, became masterpieces of private devotion—Scripture, calendar, art, and prayer woven together in one radiant object.

2. Late Gothic Architecture

Cathedrals continued to rise, now with even more intricate tracery, soaring spires, and delicate stonework that seemed almost weightless. Twilight did not end building; it transformed it.

3. The Golden Age of Polyphony

Music reached new depth.
Composers layered voices in interwoven harmonies, creating

beauty that carried both sorrow and hope. The choirs of Europe became laboratories of emotion, expressing the ache and endurance of a wounded—but believing—civilization.

Music in this age often carried a yearning tone, as if the soul of Christendom were singing through its cracks.

4. Devotional Literature

Books like *The Cloud of Unknowing* and *The Imitation of Christ* guided believers into deeper intimacy with God. These works became the spiritual companions of generations, carrying the wisdom of the age into the centuries that followed.

Even as structures trembled, the interior life of the Church grew richer.

In this twilight, God raised up voices of startling clarity.
Catherine of Siena spoke boldly to popes, calling for reform and holiness. Julian of Norwich, in the wake of plague, proclaimed one of the most hopeful visions in Christian history: "All shall be well, and all shall be well, and all manner of thing shall be well."

The mystics did not abandon the Church—they deepened it. Their writings glowed with a confidence that outshone institutional turmoil.

They represented the eternal spring rising beneath winter's frost.

Reform was not yet institutional, but it was profoundly spiritual.

Gradually, questions about authority, Scripture, and purity of life grew louder. These were not the angry cries of rebellion but the earnest pleas of believers yearning for renewal.

- **John Wycliffe** translated Scripture into English, taught that the Church must be poor in spirit, and critiqued corruption with sorrow, not malice.

- **Jan Hus**, a Czech preacher, called for integrity in leadership and devotion in the people. He was condemned and executed in 1415, yet his courage ignited longing for holiness across Central Europe.

These voices were the **early tremors before the hinge**, not the hinge itself. They showed both the need for reform and the desire for it.

As the fifteenth century advanced, Europe found itself in a strange tension: the old world was weakening, the new world was not yet born.

- kings centralized power

- economies shifted

- cities grew

- learning expanded

- printing emerged—multiplying Scripture and ideas

- classical texts resurfaced, nudging the mind toward new questions

- faith remained, but trust in certain structures waned

The harmony of the High Middle Ages did not collapse—it thinned.

Christendom still prayed, sang, built, studied, and cared for the poor.
But the unity that once felt effortless now required effort.

The moral and spiritual fabric was loosening thread by thread.

This was not rebellion against God.

It was the slow unraveling of a civilization that had carried the Gospel faithfully for centuries—and now stood in need of renewal.

By 1500, Europe stood on the edge of a hinge-point.
The world of monks, cathedrals, and harmonious Christendom had given birth to profound beauty—but also to new tensions, new questions, and new longings.

A dawn was coming, but dawn often breaks through shadows.

The Breaking Twilight was not the fall of Christendom.
It was the preparation of its heart.

The longing that would drive renewal began here:
in sorrow, in beauty, in questioning, in devotion, and in quiet
endurance.

Christ still reigned—but now the world waited for His light in
a new way.

It dims, but it does not die.

Chapter 9: The Cracks Form (1500–1600 A.D.)

When unity breaks, truth scatters like seed.

"Professing themselves to be wise, they became fools."
—Romans 1:22

By the fifteenth century, Christendom had reached its greatest height—and its limit. The harmony that had shaped Europe for a thousand years still held, but tension ran beneath the surface. The world was waking to new horizons. Knowledge expanded, culture blossomed, and human dignity—long affirmed by the Gospel—began to turn its gaze inward. Light revealed beauty, but it also revealed the first cracks in the great house of faith.

The Renaissance rekindled wonder for God's creation. Artists studied the body with reverence; scholars recovered ancient texts; architects rediscovered proportion. The world felt newly illuminated. Yet this light, once focused upward, now bent subtly toward humanity itself.

The dignity faith had given mankind matured into self-confidence. Admiration of creation became admiration of the creature. The age of harmony edged toward the age of ambition. None of it was rebellion—yet. It was the first long breath of a civilization beginning to measure by compass as well as by cross.

In this era, beauty reached new refinement. Painters like Fra Angelico blended devotion and realism. Composers wove emotion into sacred polyphony. Sculptors captured the nobility of the human face.

Art did not abandon faith; it explored it from new angles. But as the century progressed, the balance shifted. Reason asked questions once left to revelation. Curiosity reached outward and inward at once. The world was stretching.

Then a quiet revolution began. Around 1450, Johann Gutenberg developed movable type. Books multiplied. Literacy spread. Scripture could be held in a single hand.

The printing press would become one of the great tools of the Spirit—and one of the great accelerators of crisis. Truth that once flowed along a single river now branched into streams.

Erasmus of Rotterdam, scholar and reformer of the heart, stood at the threshold of the age. He edited the Greek New Testament, called for humility, and sought renewal without rupture. He loved the Church, critiqued its failings, and believed learning could heal what pride had wounded.

He was the last great voice of unity before the cracks widened.

In 1517, Martin Luther set out to debate abuses that troubled him. His Ninety-Five Theses were an invitation to reform, not rebellion. But the world was ready to move.

The hammer that struck Wittenberg's door echoed across Europe—through printing presses, universities, courts, and common homes. What began as a call to repentance became a transformation deeper and wider than any single person intended.

Scripture opened in new languages. Preachers proclaimed the Gospel with renewed urgency. The hunger for purity intensified.

But unity strained. What had once been a single choir became competing voices. Kings used reform for their own ambitions. Princes saw opportunity where theologians saw truth.

The Church's failings—real and painful—mixed with political interests and human passion. The result was not simple correction, but fragmentation.

In Germany, city by city shifted allegiance. In France, faith became entangled with civil strife. In England, the crown claimed spiritual authority, combining loyalty and loss. In Switzerland, reform marched in rival directions.

The House of Faith did not collapse, but its walls trembled. Cracks widened between believers who still prayed to the same Christ.

Throughout the sixteenth century, Europe bled—but not only from swords. It bled from:

- pride dressed as piety,

- tradition hardened into fear,

- truth spoken without charity,

- ambition masked as zeal.

Towns changed confessions with their rulers. Families divided along doctrine. Books and bodies burned together. Every side carried both conviction and blindness.

Yet even in conflict, God raised up saints. Some sought peace when peace seemed impossible. Some held firm without hatred. Some endured persecution with grace.

The Gospel was never defeated—it simply flowed through narrower channels. Rome responded not only with force but with purification.

The Council of Trent: from 1545 to 1563, bishops and theologians gathered to:

- correct abuses,

- clarify doctrine,

- renew discipline,

- restore dignity to worship.

It was a long, arduous work—imperfect yet earnest.
The Church did not rewrite the faith; it re-anchored it.

Ignatius Loyola formed the Society of Jesus, disciplined in prayer, education, and mission. They taught in universities, traveled across continents, and evangelized with clarity and courage. Where confusion had spread, they brought form. Where chaos had grown, they brought order.

Baroque as a Counter-Sermon

Art and music entered a new era of emotion and grandeur. Caravaggio's light sliced into shadow. Composers shaped sound into devotion. Churches became spaces of awe rather than argument.

Beauty pushed back against doubt.

While Europe argued, its ships encircled the earth.

Mission and Empire

Explorers carried the cross on their sails—but also the ambitions of kings.

Missionaries preached Christ with courage and tenderness.
But merchants plundered. Conquest wounded.
Faith spread through both grace and grief.

The Gospel reached the Americas, Africa, and Asia.
New believers rose in lands that had never heard the name of Jesus. But the vessels were flawed, and the voyage mixed heaven's hope with human sin.

The world was becoming one stage, but not one heart.

In 1527 came a symbolic blow:

the sack of Rome by troops who called themselves Christian.

For days, the Eternal City was pillaged. Altars desecrated, relics scattered, homes destroyed. The great house of Western faith was wounded by its own children.

Yet even there, amid smoke and sorrow:

- monks rescued manuscripts,

- believers prayed in ruined chapels,

- candles burned in hidden rooms.

The Word survived the judgment of its own generation.

Amid the turmoil, a small group of English exiles in Geneva printed a modest book in 1560: **the Geneva Bible.**

It was:

- portable,

- clear,

- translated for the common believer,

- printed for households rather than altars.

Its marginal notes taught that God alone is sovereign, and that conscience stands above kings. It became the Bible of pilgrims, reformers, refugees, and dreamers.

The Word, once bound in monasteries, became a companion for ordinary homes.

This little book carried a quiet strain of liberty that would echo in centuries to come.

By the end of the sixteenth century, the world had changed.

Reason began to stand apart from revelation.
Not yet opposed—but independent.

Questions that once belonged to theology now moved into philosophy. Human inquiry accelerated, sometimes outpacing humility.

New continents, new skies, new scientific insights widened the map of human thought. Wonder grew—but so did self-assurance.

The restraint that had shaped the medieval world loosened. Not because faith died—but because mankind began testing its strength apart from the Word.

The old order had cracked, and through those cracks new light—and new shadows—entered.

Christendom's unity shattered, but truth did not.

It scattered—like seed.

Some seeds fell on soil rich with devotion.
Some on fields hardened by pride.

Some on new continents where churches would soon rise.
Some on hearts ready for awakening.
Some on ears not yet ready to hear.

The fragmentation of the age was real.
Nations stood apart.
Doctrines diverged.
War scarred the land.

Yet amid all this, the pattern held:

- Humility separated from hubris.

- Light from shadow.

- Wheat from weed.

- Faith from fear.

The Kingdom was not collapsing—it was dividing.
A purification was underway, though few recognized its meaning.

By 1600, the medieval world was gone.
A new age—unbound, uncertain, brilliant, and perilous—stood at the threshold.

The House of Faith cracked, but its foundation remained the Word.

Chapter 10: The Season of Man (1600–1800 A.D.)

When the creature crowns itself creator.

"Ye shall be as gods." —Genesis 3:5

"Ever learning, and never able to come to the knowledge of the truth."
—2 Timothy 3:7

The thousand-year reign of Christ's influence had built a world shaped by Scripture—ordered, patient, and luminous. But as the seventeenth century dawned, the spirit of the age shifted. The restraint that had steadied the world began to loosen, not at once, but like a slow change in the wind. The memory of Christ still anchored conscience, but the gaze of mankind turned increasingly inward. A new season began— the Season of Man—when the creature admired his own reflection more than his Maker.

The Enlightenment did not arrive as rebellion, but as confidence. "I think, therefore I am" became the new cornerstone of certainty, placing the human mind where earlier ages had placed God. Descartes did not deny the divine; he simply made the self the starting point. It was a quiet movement of the center, a shift in weight that future generations would feel more sharply than he intended. In salons and lecture halls, reason rose patiently, calmly, and with growing authority. God was not rejected—only relocated to the margins, a distant architect rather than the living Lord of history.

Even so, there was real light in the new dawn. Science flourished with unprecedented brilliance. Galileo traced the paths of planets. Kepler saw in their orbits the handiwork of a God who loved order. Newton described a universe knit together by elegant laws, still believing in the Lawgiver who wrote them. Pascal, torn between faith and logic, built from both the foundations of probability and the cry of the human heart. For a time, the discoveries of science drew the mind upward in wonder. But gradually, the humility of "The heavens declare the glory of God" softened into the self-assurance of a world that found the cosmos intelligible and therefore believed itself sovereign over it.

Knowledge grew unmoored from worship. Inquiry, once an act of praise, became an act of pride. Nature was no longer seen as creation, but as machinery; humanity, no longer a steward, but an engineer. It was not open revolt—it was drift. The slow acceptance of a universe that needed God less in its daily imagination. The serpent's ancient promise found new phrasing, but the same allure: You shall be as gods.

Revolutions soon followed, shaped by this new confidence. In England, civil war toppled a king and redefined authority, yet still spoke the language of Scripture. Across the sea, the American colonies declared independence in 1776—not denying God, but claiming His sovereignty as the source of human rights. It was an imperfect experiment, but one rooted in conscience: liberty under God, freedom ordered by covenant, a new society born with the Geneva Bible in its hands.

But in France, the spirit moved differently. By 1789 the Revolution proclaimed liberty, equality, and fraternity—while cutting the cords that bound them to truth. Altars were overturned. Churches were seized. Priests fled or died. In the Cathedral of Notre Dame, the "Goddess of Reason" stood where saints once knelt. What began with hope descended into terror. Liberty without humility became violence without restraint. A nation that sought to claim the fruits of Christian morality while uprooting its foundations found itself reaping confusion instead.

Yet even as Europe strained, the Word advanced. Jesuits carried the Gospel into China, exchanging mathematics for access to imperial courts. Moravians sailed to the Caribbean, preaching Christ among those the world enslaved. Missionaries crossed oceans to Africa, India, and the Pacific. Pilgrims planted Scripture in the soil of the New World. While Europe argued over systems of thought, the faith quietly rooted itself across the globe. The Kingdom's growth did not depend on the stability of kings.

But the tools that once spread the Gospel now served competing masters. The printing press, which had placed Bibles in common hands, now carried pamphlets of skepticism. Newspapers promoted philosophies that promised progress without repentance. Education expanded

—yet often excluded the very truth that had given birth to the schools themselves. The Enlightenment looked like dawn, but its light lacked warmth; it illuminated the mind while leaving the soul chilled, ever learning yet never arriving at the knowledge of truth.

Art revealed the same shift. The Baroque age had united splendor with devotion, filling churches with movement, light, and awe. But as the eighteenth century matured, Neoclassicism displaced mystery with symmetry. Beauty remained, but its center moved. Bach composed for the glory of God; later composers wrote for the glory of the human spirit. Cathedrals still stood, but concert halls grew in number. Imagination turned its gaze from heaven to humanity, and creativity followed the arc of its age.

And still, Christ was not absent. His reign had not failed. The loosening was not defeat—it was sorting. Under persecution, faith had been tested by fear; under prosperity, it would be tested by pride. The field of humanity had expanded across continents, and once again the harvest ripened unseen. Revival flickered in small gatherings. Pietists prayed in hidden rooms. Wesley preached in fields to the forgotten. Edwards called the heart back to awe. While the mighty exalted reason, the humble rediscovered grace.

By the end of the eighteenth century, the pattern was clear. Man had gained the world—science, industry, revolution, philosophy—but the soul of Christendom had thinned. Power shifted from altar to assembly, from Scripture to speculation, from revelation to reason. The Kingdom still lived in hearts and homes, but the public imagination drifted. The age of man had begun constructing systems higher than Babel, confident that human brilliance could accomplish what only God sustains.

The world entered a new century strengthened in knowledge, restless in spirit, and quietly unanchored from the Word that once ordered its days.

Reason took the throne, faith dimmed, and the long season of testing began.

Chapter 11: The Age of Empires (1800–1914 A.D.)

When the world unites in pride, not in truth.

"The pride of thine heart hath deceived thee." —Obadiah 1:3

The nineteenth century marched beneath banners of progress. Steam crossed continents, iron spanned oceans, and nations raced to claim the world's edges as their own. Railways carved through wilderness, telegraphs stitched cities together with lines of copper, and factory chimneys replaced steeples on the skyline. It was an age of astonishing invention —and astonishing confidence. The same hands that built locomotives and laid cables also built empires. Science cured disease but bred arrogance; reason abolished superstition but enthroned materialism. The Gospel traveled with the colonizers, sometimes in love, sometimes in pride. Missionaries planted churches even as merchants plundered coasts. It was a century when the world drew close, not around the Word, but around its own ambition.

Industry became the new god—its priests in factories, its incense coal smoke. The Sabbath yielded to the schedule; children worked where choirs once sang. Cities swelled with crowds who traded the rhythms of village church bells for the relentless tempo of machines. Wealth glittered, and the poor multiplied. The Word spoke of rest and of limits, but progress rarely listened. A world that had once measured itself by altars now measured itself by output.

The arts reflected the tension. Romantic poets sought beauty amid the soot, longing for forests, mountains, and a purity the cities could not give. Even faith itself began to appear in paintings as nostalgia—a memory of candles in stone chapels, of saints and shepherds fading behind the smoke of trains. Later, realists turned their gaze to factories, slums, and fields soaked with the cost of advancement. Painters and novelists dissected a civilization that had traded wonder for efficiency. The new "higher critics" dissected Scripture with similar tools, treating the Bible as just another ancient text. In some universities, revelation became a subject, not a source. The age probed everything, including the faith that had birthed it.

Yet light never vanished entirely. The Great Awakenings swept through Britain and America, stirring hearts that factories could not satisfy. Wesley and Whitefield left their mark on earlier decades; now preachers like Charles Spurgeon thundered in London, and Moody preached across continents. Songs of praise rose from crowded halls and open fields, reminding multitudes that the cross still stood above the smokestacks. Missionaries spread through India, Africa, Asia, and the islands—carrying Bibles in one hand, sometimes medicine in the other. They preached Christ to kings and tribes, to plantation workers and prisoners. Some came as servants, loving the people they met; others arrived entangled in the prejudices of their age. The same ships that carried the slave trade now sometimes carried those who opposed it. The Gospel was present in both the sin and the repentance of the century.

The world knit itself together with wires and rails. Telegraph lines connected capitals; railways shrank continents; steamships made oceans feel like wide rivers. Messages that once took months now traveled in minutes. Trade boomed. Armies moved faster. News of revival reached distant coasts; news of war and revolution did as well. The Church adjusted slowly, sending missionaries along these new routes, printing tracts on new presses, and gathering offerings in new currencies. Christ's Word rode the same systems that also carried ideologies opposed to Him.

Nationalism swelled alongside progress. Old kingdoms reassembled themselves into new nations—Italy, Germany, and others—fueled by dreams of unity and dominance. Flags multiplied, and with them the conviction that each nation carried a unique destiny. Some wrapped that destiny in Christian language; others invoked race, history, or blood. Underneath the rhetoric, pride grew. Empires claimed continents as if they were empty, carving borders with rulers across maps. The peoples who lived inside those lines seldom had a voice. The language of "civilizing" masked greed; the rhetoric of "uplift" often rode on the back of exploitation.

Ideas about humanity hardened in dangerous ways. Darwin's observations about life were twisted into "social Darwinism," teaching that the strong deserved to rule the weak. This logic baptized cruelty in the name of science. The poor, the colonized, and the conquered were told their suffering was natural, even beneficial. It was a quiet betrayal of the Gospel's insistence that the last shall be first and that the least are most precious in God's sight.

Even theology felt the pressure. In some pulpits, faith softened into mere morality, a gentle religion of respectability. In others, it broke into protest—voices demanding justice for workers, women, and slaves. The Bible inspired both comfort and confrontation. New movements arose—Holiness revivals, early Pentecostal stirrings near the century's end—pointing back to the living power of the Spirit in an age that thought itself too sophisticated for miracles. God did not abandon the world to its machines; He moved through them, calling hearts home in unexpected places.

By century's end, the world was global and restless. Maps were nearly full; seas thoroughly charted. Telegraphs pulsed across continents. Newspapers reported wars and revivals side by side. Missionary societies sent reports from remote villages; stock markets speculated on resources extracted from those same lands. The dream of human unity seemed within reach. World's Fairs displayed inventions and cultures under one roof, promising a future of shared progress. Peace conferences spoke of law among nations. It all seemed so near—an ordered world, rational and prosperous.

Yet beneath the polished surface, cracks ran deep. Colonized peoples simmered under foreign flags. Workers seethed in crowded tenements. Armies grew larger, armed with weapons no previous age had imagined. Alliances formed like invisible tripwires across Europe. Pride and fear walked together, smiling for the cameras at expositions, brooding in war rooms and cabinets. Prayer meetings continued, but their sound was nearly drowned by the hum of industry and the applause of progress.

In the twilight of the 1800s, the world stood poised on the edge of greatness and judgment. The harvest of reason and empire had come full circle; wealth and technology encircled the globe, and confidence filled the air. The tower of man stood tall again, built this time not from bricks on a plain, but from factories, flags, and philosophies. Heaven watched, not surprised. The world had united in pride, not in truth.

The stage was set. The Age of Empires had reached its shimmering height, and just beyond its horizon, a storm gathered that no invention could divert and no empire could command.

Chapter 12: The Age of Fire (1914–1945 A.D.)

When the world is tested by flame.

"For nation shall rise against nation, and kingdom against kingdom: there shall be famines, and pestilences, and earthquakes in divers places."
—Matthew 24:7

"The earth also was corrupt before God, and the earth was filled with violence." —Genesis 6:11

The twentieth century opened with confidence. Cities towered, factories roared, and science promised a future unmarred by the errors of the past. The same engines that carried missionaries across oceans now carried armies. Progress, once the servant of faith, began to dream of becoming its replacement. Humanity had mastered nature, and in its pride believed it had mastered itself.

The first global war was not born of famine or plague but of ambition—nations swollen with confidence, alliances knotted in secrecy, rivalries sharpened by envy. A single gunshot in Sarajevo collided with an age already leaning toward violence, and the world tipped into fire. Trenches scarred Europe like open wounds. Fields where poppies once grew became wastelands of mud, wire, and bones. Poison drifted across the land as if creation itself had turned against man. The old order—crowns, customs, and the quiet moral framework inherited from Christendom—buckled under the weight of mechanized war.

The Great War shattered more than empires; it shattered illusions. A century that had believed in moral ascent discovered that knowledge without wisdom leads only to more efficient destruction. Men who had sung in chapels now marched to slaughter beneath banners of nationalism and reason. The Enlightenment's hope of a rational world drowned in the trenches, leaving the soul of civilization shaken and uncertain.

When the guns fell silent in 1918, the victors proclaimed triumph, but the world felt hollowed. A pandemic swept the globe—a pestilence that claimed tens of millions, moving swiftly through weary nations unprepared for another wave of death. Churches filled not with revival but with mourning. The League of Nations arose with high ideals but lacked the humility to bind them. The restraint once provided by shared faith had thinned, and pride began its slow reconstruction.

The 1920s arrived glittering with invention and desire—jazz, automobiles, cinema, skyscrapers. The world called it the "modern age," a fresh beginning. But beneath the shimmer, the foundations cracked. Greed replaced gratitude; speculation replaced stability; the ease of prosperity masked a spiritual drought. When markets collapsed in 1929, the decade's brightness dissolved into fear. The Great Depression spread across continents, and faith in progress faltered once again.

In the vacuum, new powers rose. A wounded Germany sought redemption and found it in vengeance. Russia's revolution hardened into tyranny. Italy embraced a myth of Roman glory. Japan built an empire beneath banners of divine national destiny. Each promised salvation through strength, order through obedience, renewal through blood. Idols of the modern age—race, nation, class, destiny—took shape in the space where God had been pushed aside.

The 1930s deepened the crisis. Famines swept Ukraine. Camps expanded across Siberia. Books burned in German squares. Armies marched across Asia. A counterfeit kingdom unfurled under the swastika, demanding worship and obedience, offering belonging in exchange for the soul. Stalin's purges devoured millions. Japan's conquests brought terror to villages that had never heard the names of their invaders. Every ideology claimed to build a perfect world; each left only graves.

When war came again in 1939, it came not as a clash of nations but as a global storm. Entire cities became targets. Oceans churned with steel and fire. Civilians suffered beside soldiers. Industry—once a symbol of progress—became an altar upon which the young were sacrificed by the millions. The world plunged into a darkness deeper than any age had seen.

Then came the Holocaust: evil laid bare without disguise. Not chaos, but calculation; not madness, but method. Bureaucracy became instrument; ideology became justification; entire peoples were marked for erasure. In ghettos and camps, humanity confronted the logical end of its rebellion—the belief that man may decide who bears the right to live. It was the bitter fruit of an age that had exalted itself above God.

Yet even in the shadows, light persisted. Churches gathered in basements. Families hid the hunted. Pastors and priests risked their lives to defy tyrants. Bonhoeffer prayed and wrote from prison. Corrie ten Boom carried forgiveness into places forged by cruelty. Quiet saints rose where the world least expected them, proving that the Word had not withdrawn from history.

In 1945, the war reached its terrible climax. Scientists split the atom, releasing a power once reserved for the Creator alone. When the bombs fell on Hiroshima and Nagasaki, the sky lit with a brightness unnatural to earth. Two cities vanished in moments. For the first time, humanity held the capacity to erase itself—an authority it was never meant to bear. The age had reached the farthest boundary of pride, and mercy alone prevented the final step.

When the smoke at last cleared, the world was changed but not healed. Empires that had stood for centuries dissolved. Borders shifted. Nations rebuilt from rubble with equal parts hope and exhaustion. But peace did not feel secure; it felt conditional, fragile. The silence after the storm carried the hum of unrest.

The war had not ended so much as paused. The Beast of human pride had been wounded, but not destroyed. New lines divided the earth. The United States and the Soviet Union emerged as opposing visions—one shaped by remnants of Christian conscience, the other by enforced atheism. Missiles replaced swords; suspicion replaced diplomacy; ideology replaced faith. The world entered a colder, quieter form of conflict, its future balanced on weapons it prayed never to use.

And yet, the Word continued its quiet work. Soldiers returned home and found faith stirring in unexpected ways. Missionaries journeyed into lands reopened by the end of empire. Families prayed over ruins and rebuilt their lives. Grace moved beneath the surface of nations stunned by what they had witnessed.

The Age of Fire had purified, but it had not reconciled. It exposed the depth of human pride and the danger of a world that forgets its Maker. Judgment had burned across continents, but mercy held the world back from the brink. A new era dawned—not with relief, but with caution. Mankind had survived the furnace, yet had not repented.

The earth moved with progress once more.
Heaven heard the strain of restraint returning.

A global age had begun—an age not of fire, but of fear.

Chapter 13: The Age of Division (1945–1960 A.D.)

When fear held the world in place, but not together.

"He who now letteth will let, until he be taken out of the way."

— 2 Thessalonians 2:7

The fire had ceased, but the world still smoldered. Cities lay in ruins, nations mourned their dead, and the memory of judgment lingered like a heat that would not dissipate. Humanity vowed never again to unleash such destruction, but vows born of fear rarely endure. Survival was mistaken for salvation, and the quiet between wars was mistaken for peace.

The ancient empires were gone, their crowns dissolved into rubble and regret. In their place stood two towering powers—America and the Soviet Union—each claiming to represent the future, each convinced it bore the destiny of mankind. Their borders were not merely political lines but boundaries of belief. One upheld freedom shaped by the remnants of Christian conscience; the other built its identity on a creed that denied heaven altogether. The world divided not simply by geography, but by the unseen loyalties of the soul.

What followed was an age without open war yet without true peace. Fear became the new equilibrium. Missiles waited in silos, bombers circled the edges of continents, and military doctrines replaced diplomacy. Science reached upward with the launch of satellites, yet the heavens they entered felt colder than ever before. Humanity had touched the sky, but not its Maker.

The Iron Curtain that stretched across Europe was more than a boundary of tanks and treaties. It was a veil drawn across memory and meaning. On one side, the name of God could still be spoken aloud; on the other, it was erased from textbooks and forbidden in public squares. Churches were shuttered or turned into museums—silent monuments to a faith the state declared obsolete. Children learned that history marched forward without God, that progress was inevitable, and that the soul was an old superstition. Yet even in the places where Bibles were banned, they multiplied. Pages were copied by lamplight, verses read in prison cells, and sermons memorized because ink and paper were too dangerous.

In the West, the danger was quieter. Prosperity grew quickly in the years after the war. Families filled new neighborhoods, children filled new schools, and comfort filled the spaces where conviction once lived. Gratitude faded into assumption; dependence on God softened into formality. The television replaced the hearth, and entertainment began to shape imagination more powerfully than Scripture. Faith did not disappear—it thinned. The wheat still grew, but the weeds found easy soil.

Across the divide, persecution purified what prosperity diluted. In Soviet labor camps, believers prayed through the clatter of chains. In China, house churches gathered in secret long before dawn. In Eastern Europe, pastors preached to dwindling congregations, trusting that unseen listeners were being strengthened. The Spirit moved where liberty could not, and the Word traveled paths no government could fully block —radio waves slipping over borders, missionaries slipping into remote villages, hope slipping into hearts wearied by oppression.

Yet light did not belong only to the persecuted. In the West, revival stirred in unexpected ways. Billy Graham's early ministry spread through stadiums and radio, calling nations to repentance even as the world drifted toward distraction. Across Europe, ruins became sanctuaries as churches rebuilt stone by stone. In America, a young civil rights movement began to root itself in Scripture's insistence that all are made in the image of God. The Word continued its quiet work, even as nations measured strength by weapons instead of wisdom.

The global order that emerged after 1945 carried the appearance of stability but not the substance of peace. The restraint that held the world together was not human agreement but divine mercy—the same unseen hand that had halted judgment now holding history back from another precipice. Nations spoke of treaties, but the real balance lay in a Providence they no longer acknowledged.

By the end of the 1950s, the pattern was clear. The world was divided into two vast households, each with its own fears, its own convictions, and its own fragilities. The conflict would not be settled by armies on fields, but by ideas in minds, by loyalties in hearts. Faith would be tested not by fire this time, but by comfort and control—two forces equally capable of eroding the soul.

The Age of Division revealed a solemn truth:

peace without repentance is only postponement. The world had survived the fire, but it had not learned from it. Judgment had paused, not passed.

Beneath the calm surface of the new order, the embers of the last war still glowed—quiet, unresolved, waiting for the winds that would stir them again.

Chapter 14: The Cold Kingdom (1960–1990 A.D.)

When comfort cools the soul and courage warms the nations.

"For Satan himself is transformed into an angel of light." —2 Corinthians 11:14

The decades after the war brought prosperity no one expected. Streets once filled with rubble echoed with children's laughter. Factories reopened. Nations rebuilt. But as the physical world brightened, the spiritual climate cooled. Gratitude faded into assumption; devotion thinned into routine. A new generation inherited peace it did not fight for and abundance it did not remember living without. Comfort, once a blessing, became a blanket that muffled the voice of conscience.

By the early 1960s, the West was rich but restless. Faith continued in form, but its fire dimmed. Prayer disappeared from classrooms. The unborn were declared unwanted. Morality—once rooted in Scripture—was recast as preference. The rebellion spoken of in Eden found a new language in cities and campuses. What had begun as a protest against hypocrisy grew into a revolt against holiness itself. "I need nothing," the age declared, not seeing how poor it had become.

Yet even as the West lost its footing, the Gospel surged across the world. In Africa, fields became sanctuaries as crowds gathered beneath open sky to hear of a Savior who saw the forgotten. In Latin America, revival stirred among the poor and oppressed. In Korea, prayer mountains thundered through the night. And in China—despite raids, prisons, and persecution—the underground church multiplied faster than any could suppress. Faith left the buildings of the powerful and rooted itself among the humble, the hungry, the unseen. The Kingdom moved quietly but decisively.

Meanwhile, the world's great ideological struggle hardened. The Cold War continued its tense vigil, but the nature of the conflict had shifted. It was no longer defined by battle lines but by worldviews—freedom strained by indulgence, and atheistic control strained by its own emptiness. Across the Iron Curtain, citizens lived beneath a creed that denied heaven and rewrote history. Churches were surveilled, pastors imprisoned, Scripture outlawed. Children memorized slogans instead of psalms. Hope was monitored; conscience was a threat. And yet, beneath the frost, seeds survived. Believers met in basements, prayed in stairwells and smuggled Bibles under sacks of grain. The underground Church grew like roots beneath winter soil—hidden, patient, preparing for spring.

The West faced a different coldness—one not imposed by force but invited by desire. Entertainment replaced meditation. Screens replaced silence. Fashion replaced virtue. The soul, no longer pressed by hardship, drifted into distraction. It was a polite decline, gentle but steady. People were not hostile to God; they simply lived as if they no longer needed Him. Churches remained standing, but many hearts inside felt hollow. The idols of the age were pleasant, luminous, and celebrated—angels of light, bearing promises of freedom that slowly tightened into chains.

Yet God did not withdraw. In the 1970s and 80s, a quiet spiritual hunger returned. The Jesus Movement swept through youth disillusioned by war and materialism. Evangelists filled stadiums with the call to repentance. Missionaries fanned across continents newly open to the Gospel. Even in the West's indifference, sparks of longing glowed. The Word worked around the obstacles comfort had created.

Meanwhile, in the East, courage awakened. Truth began to seep through the cracks in the Soviet facade. Economies faltered. Lies unraveled. Workers in Poland prayed openly in shipyards, forming movements that shook empires. In Russia, believers gathered without fear for the first time in decades. Pastors long silenced preached again to crowds hungry for hope. Hymns rose where propaganda once echoed. What had been frozen for generations began to thaw.

By the late 1980s, the Cold Kingdom was collapsing under its own weight. Walls that once seemed immovable trembled. Ideologies that demanded worship proved hollow. Nations long held in darkness lifted their heads. In 1989, the Berlin

Wall fell—not to armies, but to candles, prayers, and a longing that no state could extinguish. People crossed freely, weeping, singing songs of freedom as stones tumbled around them. It was a moment when history revealed its deeper Author—when grace broke through concrete.

But even as one empire of control fell, another began to rise —quieter, subtler, clothed not in steel but in screens. Technology, once a servant, was becoming a shaper. Information traveled faster than wisdom. Voices multiplied faster than truth. Isolation grew even amid connection. Ideologies flowed through wires instead of borders. The next kingdom would not require soldiers to conquer; it would require attention. The new chains would be invisible.

By 1990, the world celebrated peace, unaware that a different kind of battle had already begun. The Cold War ended, but the coldness did not. Hearts remained restless, nations remained proud, and the foundation beneath modern life trembled with unseen cracks.

The Cold Kingdom had cracked and crumbled, but the chill it left behind remained. The walls fell, yet new shadows stretched across the earth—silent, luminous, inviting.

The world entered the age of distraction

Chapter 15: The Digital Dominion (1990–2015 A.D.)

When the world connected—and the soul drifted.

"The lofty looks of Man shall be humbled and the haughtiness of men shall be bowed down, and the Lord alone shall be exalted in that day."
—Isaiah 2:11

"He causeth all, both small and great, rich and poor, free and bond, to receive a mark."

—Revelation 13:16

When the cold kingdom cracked and fell, it collapsed not with bombs but with candles and prayers. Walls crumbled, crowds sang in the streets, and iron gates opened that had been locked for generations. In the squares of Moscow, people spoke the name of God aloud again, their breath hanging in the winter air like a long-forgotten song. The world rejoiced, believing tyranny had been broken once and for all. Freedom walked where fear had ruled, and hope rose from the dust of fallen statues.

Yet the fall of the Soviet empire was more than the end of a regime. It was the quiet unraveling of a power that had tried to silence heaven. Like Babel, it had built its identity on the absence of God; like Babel, it fell by its own weight. No foreign army had conquered it. Truth had. The prayers of the persecuted outlasted the prisons meant to erase them. Believers who had read Scripture in cellars and camps were now standing in daylight, their faith unshaken, their courage undiminished. The Kingdom had advanced not with force, but through endurance.

History's pattern echoed again: every people who exalt themselves against Him eventually face their own undoing. Jerusalem rejected the Messiah and fell within a generation, its Temple reduced to memory and its people scattered. Babylon mocked the holy vessels and collapsed overnight. Rome fed Christians to lions and was later reshaped by their Gospel. Germany attempted to erase God's chosen people; its own darkness devoured itself. Japan enthroned a human emperor as divine; the illusion shattered under fire. The Soviet Union raised atheism as its creed; its own contradictions pulled it down. Each tried to silence the Word—each became a caution rather than a kingdom.

The early 1990s felt like morning after a long night. Nations newly freed opened their doors to missionaries. Bibles crossed borders once patrolled by soldiers. Churches rebuilt in places that had forgotten the sound of hymns. It seemed, for a moment, that the world might breathe again, might remember its Maker. The Cold War ended without total ruin, and humanity mistook mercy for mastery.

But restraint removed reveals what fear had hidden. Without the threat of war pressing on conscience, a new temptation rose—subtle, soft, and deeply appealing. The world embraced amusement. Instead of ideology, distraction. Instead of tyranny, self. The battlefields of the twentieth century gave way to the comforts of the twenty-first.

In America, prosperity bloomed. The economy soared, churches filled, missionaries went to nations once closed, and the Bible was translated into languages no empire had ever reached. Yet abundance carries its own shadows. The more the nation gained, the less it seemed to remember why it had been blessed. Gratitude slowly thinned. Entertainment became constant. The market shaped desire more than Scripture shaped conscience. It was not rebellion so much as drift—quiet, steady, unintentional.

Then, in 1991—the same year the Soviet Union fell—the World Wide Web was born. What began as a tool of communication quickly grew into a new kind of dominion: borderless, tireless, invisible. It promised connection, efficiency, and limitless knowledge. And in many ways, it delivered wonders: families reunited by messages, students informed by oceans of learning, missionaries supported by instant communication. But every blessing carries a warning, and this one was woven into its very design.

The internet became something built not from brick or stone, but from something else. It rose without architects, without kings, without borders. It crossed every ocean without leaving a wake. At first, it served humanity. Then humanity began to serve it. Knowledge multiplied, but wisdom thinned. Information increased, but understanding weakened. A generation that could access anything struggled to hear anything that mattered.

A new kind of empire emerged—an empire not of nations but of attention. Its rulers were unseen, its citizens willingly bound. Convenience became creed. Self-expression became virtue. Privacy, once a treasure, became optional. Human beings, connected more than ever, felt more isolated than before. The body sat free in living rooms and cafés, but the mind wandered tethered to a glowing screen.

The digital dominion did not demand loyalty by force. It invited it with ease. It shaped belief not with decrees but with suggestions. Algorithms—silent, tireless, precise—became the new teachers, curating what people saw, heard, and eventually thought. The screens that promised liberation also fostered longing, comparison, distraction, and a subtle erosion of stillness. The world grew louder as the soul grew quieter.

And yet, amid the rise of the new age, the Word did not retreat. It moved through these same networks—through online sermons, digital Bibles, global worship, and voices of faith reaching places missionaries could not travel. Children in remote villages watched stories of Jesus on tiny screens. Families in closed nations found Scripture hidden in code. The same system that spread confusion carried light into corners untouched by any prior era.

The Digital Dominion was neither wholly dark nor wholly bright. It was a mirror—reflecting the heart of a world newly connected and newly divided, brilliantly informed yet deeply unsure. The age that believed it had stepped into the future had, in truth, stepped into another threshold: a place where man's reach exceeded his grounding, where voices multiplied faster than truth, and where the battle for the soul shifted into realms no prior generation had faced.

And once again, the world would learn that every tower —digital or stone—reveals the heart of its builders.

Chapter 16: The Age of Delusion (2015–Present)

When reality can be chosen, truth becomes optional.

"Because they received not the love of the truth… God shall send them strong delusion, that they should believe a lie."

—2 Thessalonians 2:10–11

"Woe unto them that call evil good, and good evil; that put darkness for light, and light for darkness…"

—Isaiah 5:20

The modern world feels peaceful, but its quiet is misleading. The nations that once trembled under war now bask in comfort; the technologies that once carried the Gospel across oceans now carry distraction into every home. Knowledge floods the earth, brighter and faster than lightning, yet truth feels dimmer than ever. People live longer, work less, and want more. Fear has faded, but discernment has faded with it. The danger of this age is not chaos—it is calm.

The delusion of our time does not shout; it soothes. It whispers that humanity has outgrown its need for God, that progress is enough, that goodness is whatever we feel, that truth is whatever we choose. It promises a world without guilt, without limits, without absolutes. A world where every desire can be affirmed and every disagreement avoided. A world without sin because everything is permitted. Darkness does not invade—people simply stop noticing when the lights dim.

In earlier ages, men bowed to idols made of stone. Now they bow to the self. The oldest temptation—"You shall be as gods"—has become a cultural creed. Identity is no longer something received; it is something constructed. Meaning is no longer discovered; it is invented. The self is treated as sacred, and its impulses as divine. The cross still hangs in churches, but its call to surrender sounds foreign in a world taught that fulfillment lies in indulgence. The delusion of this age is not that God is denied; it is that He is replaced—quietly, politely, with ourselves.

Meanwhile, science has risen from servant to interpreter of meaning. Its achievements are real and remarkable: medicines that cure, technologies that connect, but somewhere along the way, wonder became control. Laboratories promise to erase suffering, edit genomes, and extend life. Engineers speak of minds uploaded, consciousness digitized, humanity upgraded —until progress itself becomes salvation—the question of the soul becomes obsolete. The danger is not in the breakthroughs themselves, but in the belief that they render God unnecessary.

Yet the greatest shift of this age is not moral or technological —it is perceptual. For the first time in history, reality has become customizable. Screens now shape vision more than sight does. What a person sees, hears, and believes is no longer shared but curated. Every mind lives inside its own personalized world, crafted by invisible algorithms that learn its habits, and desires. News comes tailored, truth filtered, outrage preselected. Two neighbors look at the same event and see different worlds. The foundation of shared reality, once assumed, dissolves.

Entertainment has crossed a threshold too. It no longer reflects the world; it replaces it. A person's appearance can be altered beyond recognition. Faces can be generated, voices imitated, memories edited. News will routinely blur fiction and fact. Virtual worlds promise whatever version of reality the user prefers. Soon, one could watch a soccer match and choose the outcome—victory, defeat, or spectacle—depending on the emotion he wishes to feel. When reality itself becomes optional, truth becomes disposable.

In such a world, community falters. People gather online, yet feel profoundly alone. They scroll endlessly through curated lives, comparing themselves to illusions that were never meant to be lived. Anxiety rises in the most comfortable societies ever recorded. Depression grows where abundance should satisfy. Hearts starve amid full pantries. The soul, created for eternal things, weakens under the weight of momentary pleasures. Noise fills every waking moment, until silence—where God's voice dwells—feels unbearable.

Faith, too, feels the strain. Scripture is quoted, softened, revised, and reshaped to fit the spirit of the age. Truth is treated as flexible, conviction as intolerance. Some pulpits exchange repentance for affirmation, holiness for sentiment, discipleship for brand identity. The Gospel becomes another product in the marketplace of ideas, competing for attention rather than calling for transformation. Few reject Christ outright, but many reshape Him into a more palatable image. God is tolerated so long as He does not contradict the self.

And yet, even here, the pattern of history remains unchanged: whenever delusion spreads, the remnant awakens. In small churches, rural towns, and quiet apartments, faith rekindles. Families pray. Believers rediscover Scripture not as a slogan but as sustenance. Young people weary of noise seek silence again. Worship rises without lights or stages. The Spirit works in the margins, as He always has—steady, gentle, persistent.

The world stands on the edge of a new age—one not built of stone or steel, but of data, convenience, and curated identity. Global systems synchronize. Technology becomes intimate, invisible, formative. The promise is safety and ease; the price is the soul's attention. It is the same ancient pattern with modern polish: a kingdom built without God, offered with a smile.

But delusion never has the final word. Beneath the glow of the screens, beneath the sound of progress, beneath the numbness of distraction, the Kingdom still grows. Quietly. Person to person, heart to heart. The darkness of this age is subtle, but the Light remains unchanged and it still speaks for those who will listen. Even the tools that confuse the world can clarify the Word when placed in God's hands. Technology is not the enemy of truth; it becomes its servant when guided by a faithful heart. The truth still stands for those who seek it.

This age is not the end—it is the test.
And the darkness has not overcome it.

Chapter 17: The Remnant Rises

When the few remember what the many forget.

"They that know their God shall be strong, and do exploits." —
Daniel 11:32

"Fear not, little flock; for it is your Father's good pleasure to give you the kingdom." —Luke 12:32

Beneath the sounds of endless noise and the glow of a thousand screens, something small and steady began to stir. Not a movement, not a trend—something older and quieter. It rose in places the age of delusion overlooks: in kitchens after dinner, in silent prayers at bedside, in small congregations. The faith that had long been pushed to the margins found that God was waiting there.

History has always hinged on the faithful few. Not the powerful or the polished, but the willing. When nations exalted themselves, God preserved. When empires hardened their hearts, He spoke to prophets in deserts. Every age of confusion has given birth to a remnant—those who see clearly when the world blurs. This age is no different.

The remnant does not rise with fanfare. It rises with endurance. They are not united by nation or denomination, but by hunger—an ache for what is real in a world of curated illusions. They gather in living rooms, barns, basements, and forests. In Africa and Asia, believers meet by candlelight under the watch of hostile eyes. In the West, families rediscover the strength of prayer after work Scripture read slowly, faith practiced simply. Children memorize verses their schools would never dare speak. Others pray for a generation lost in the glow of its own devices.

Their revival is not a spectacle; it is a returning. Not loud, but lasting. Not viral, but vital. It takes root in the cracks of a weary culture and grows in hidden soil.

The remnant lives differently. They trade noise for silence, comparison for contentment, excess for simplicity. They remember the ancient rhythms that once formed saints— fasting, prayer, Scripture, service. In a world chasing applause, they prefer anonymity. In an age of instant outrage, they practice patience. They choose faithfulness in small things, unseen things, ordinary things. And these choices—small but costly—begin to change everything around them.

Their faith is not comfortable, but courageous. They speak truth without anger, love without compromise, forgive without applause. Some lose jobs for integrity, friendships for honesty, opportunities for conscience. Yet their losses become testimonies. Their peace confounds the anxious age. They are not anxious about the shifting world because they belong to a Kingdom that does not shift.

Across continents and cultures, the Spirit weaves these quiet believers into a living tapestry. Ordinary people who have simply learned to listen again. They hear a different voice beneath the roar of the age. They recognize the Shepherd's call in the still places where truth has not been drowned out. They sense that the world is tightening, that the illusions are thinning, that history is bending toward a point—but they do not fear. They prepare.

God has always begun renewal with the remnant. He preserved a family through a flood, a prophet through famine, a nation through exile, the Church through persecution. He does not need crowds—He needs faith. And faith has never been measured by numbers, but by obedience.

The next awakening will not begin on stages or in stadiums. It will begin in prayer. In hospital rooms, in confessions, and in unexpected acts of mercy. It will not trend, but it will transform. It will not be televised, but it will be true. The remnant carries no banners but love, no ambition but holiness, no strength but the Spirit. They rebuild what pride destroyed—not with power, but with patience.

Even now, as global systems rise and identities blur and nations tremble in confusion, the real Kingdom grows unseen. It cannot be censored, digitized, or manipulated. It is written not on servers but on souls. It does not demand attention; it invites allegiance. It does not promise ease; it offers peace. And the remnant, small though they may be, carry this Kingdom forward with steady hands.

To the reader who longs for clarity in a world of curated truths, the call is simple: awaken. Return to the silence where God still speaks. Turn from the self that promises freedom but delivers burden. Let go of the delusion that progress can replace presence. The Spirit still searches for those willing to stand in the gap, to live faithfully when faith is unfashionable, to choose holiness when compromise is easy, to carry the Word where the world has turned its ears away.

The remnant is not a club or a movement. It is a way of being. A posture of humility in an age of pride. A life of truth in a world of preference. A flame kept burning in a wind that tries to extinguish it. And when the towers of this age finally fall—as all towers do—it will be the remnant who rise to rebuild.

For though the world forgets the Word, the Word never forgets the world.

Chapter 18: The Return

When history's echo becomes a voice again.

"Heaven and earth shall pass away, but My words shall not pass away." — Matthew 24:35

The noise of the age will not endure. The screens will dim, the systems will strain, the monuments of pride will fracture as they always have. The engines of progress, the illusions of control—they will fade like breath on glass. Every empire built on human brilliance dissolves when the wind changes. But the Word remains. It stood before nations existed, and it will stand when nations are only names in the margins of memory.

History is a long record of voices trying to rise higher than God's—and every time, He answers not with argument, but with endurance. When human noise grows unbearable, divine silence becomes unmistakable. The world does not end in chaos; it ends in clarity. When the world exhausts its own wisdom, the whisper of the Spirit can finally be heard again.

From the Word spoken at creation, to Him being made flesh, to His message written upon hearts—this has always been His story. The rise and fall of kingdoms, the brilliance and blindness of ages, the widening and narrowing of history—all of it has been the rhythm of revelation. Triumph revealed His mercy; judgment revealed His holiness; endurance revealed His truth. Every empire that fell cracked open a seal. Every persecution refined His people. Every age of pride uncovered its own futility. And through it all, God has moved forward— quiet, patient, unbroken.

Now, in a world that calls illusion progress, the Spirit stirs once more. Not in palaces or platforms, but in the humble and the hungry. Not with signs of spectacle, but with the returning weight of conviction. The Kingdom is not coming the way men predict; it is emerging the way it always has— first in hearts, then in history.

Humanity has spent generations chasing its own reflection: worshiping progress, trusting systems, admiring the glow of its own inventions. But illusions have limits. They can comfort for a moment, never for a lifetime. And when illusion collapses, reality returns like dawn over a long night. Reality has a face, a name, and a voice. Christ is not returning to reclaim what was lost—He is returning to reveal what was never defeated.

The Kingdom that began at His resurrection has been growing through the centuries like a seed beneath snow. One day it will rise in full. The veil between the seen and the unseen will part again—not through suffering, but fulfillment. The same Word that once spoke light into darkness will speak again, and every false light will flicker out. Pride will watch its towers tremble. Delusion will watch its illusions collapse. Not in rage, but in mercy—for judgment is not vengeance, but restoration.

The shaking to come will not destroy the faithful—it will define them. Those who built their lives on the Rock will remain when the scaffolding of this age falls away. The storms of history have always revealed foundations more than failures.

The Lord is patient, but His patience is not permission. He has allowed man to play god so that man might see the emptiness of the role. And when every imitation fails, truth will stand alone. Not shouted, not enforced—simply revealed.

"Behold, I make all things new."

Those words will echo through creation, and nothing will silence them. What began in a garden will end in one—not as a return to innocence, but as the completion of redemption. The curse that cast its long shadow over time will lift. What was broken will be healed. What was wounded will be made whole. And the world will walk again with its Maker in unmarred light.

Scripture is not merely a record of the past; it is the architecture of the future. History itself has been commentary. The rise of civilizations, their brilliance, their blindness, their collapse—all have been the story unfolding, seal after seal, lesson after lesson. Yet the greatest revelation is not reserved for the end of time—it waits in any soul that awakens today. Every heart that turns back to God is a small resurrection. Every act of repentance restores a piece of the world. The Kingdom is not postponed; it is present, waiting to be recognized.

"Behold, I stand at the door and knock."
The age of delusion cannot silence that voice. The towers of

this world will fall, the Beast will grow weary of its own emptiness, and the Word will endure—still steady, still sovereign. The real question is not what happens to the world, but what happens within us.

The return begins not with nations, but with individuals. When a man turns off the noise long enough to hear his own soul again. When a family prays without embarrassment. When a woman forgives what the world says should never be forgiven. When a child believes that Jesus is real, even if the culture does not. Revival begins smaller than we expect—and stronger than we imagine.

The return is not political or institutional. It is personal. It begins in humility and ends in restoration. The Word is not far away; it waits in the stillness the world has forgotten how to enter.

The Spirit and the Bride still say, **Come.**

The invitation that echoed from Calvary has never been withdrawn. The gates are still open. Grace is still extended. The story is not ending—it is circling back to its beginning.

When all is shaken, one truth will remain:

The Word reigns through time. History is not the story of man searching for God, but of God revealing Himself through man's rise and fall.

The Kingdom advances and endures.

And the invitation still stands

Epilogue: The Word Beyond Time

To those still listening.

The story you've just read is not finished. It continues every time someone opens a Bible, kneels in repentance, or chooses truth when lies would be easier. History is not a record to be studied—it is a mirror held to every generation. The same forces that shaped nations still shape hearts.

Every empire that crumbled began with a single exchange: man choosing his will over God's. And every renewal began when one soul reversed that choice. The Word is not trapped in the past; it breathes through time, through language, through lives. It speaks through art, through conscience, through the quiet moments when you sense something larger than yourself calling you. That is not nostalgia—that is eternity reminding you that it is near.

The delusion of this age says you are alone, that truth is gone, that all that was sacred has been hollowed out. Do not believe it. The same Spirit that hovered over the waters still hovers over you. The same voice that spoke to prophets still speaks in the silence of your soul—if you are willing to be still long enough to listen.

Silence, however, is not only about noise. The body itself can become too loud to hear the Spirit. When the mind is clouded by intoxication or the body dulled by neglect, the inner self can't hear it. The Spirit speaks through clarity—through rest, through reverence, through discipline. To care for the vessel is to honor the voice within it. The body is not the enemy of the soul; it is its instrument. Keep it clean, and the music will sound again.

Turn off the noise. Step outside. Remember what creation sounds like without commentary. Breathe air unfiltered by fear. Eat what is alive, drink what is pure, move with purpose. Treat your life as the temple it was meant to be. Read the Bible again, slowly, as if for the first time. It is alive—not a relic, but a pulse.

You cannot change the world, but you can refuse to join its delusion. You can reclaim what was lost in small ways: a prayer before sleep, a truth spoken when silence would be safer, a kindness done without witness. These things matter more than you think. They are the seeds of the next age.

The Spirit is still writing the story—through your obedience, your endurance, your faith. Do not fear the future. The same God who held the universe in the beginning still holds it now. And when the world grows dark again, remember: darkness has never been permanent. It only sets the stage for light to be revealed.

"And the light shineth in darkness; and the darkness comprehended it not." —John 1.

So hold fast to the Word. Guard your heart and your mind, strengthen your body, and keep your spirit awake. For the soul hears best through a vessel that is clear, humble, and whole.

The Word is older than the stars, stronger than the grave, and closer than your breath. It was, and is, and is to come.

The Kingdom Revealed

We are not standing on uncertain ground.

To awaken from the man-made world is not madness—it is sight. The delusion breaks when you see that the world built on man's wisdom is the imitation, and the one formed by God's Word is the real.

When you turn from illusion—from self-worship, distraction, and the false promise that progress alone can save—you begin to see through the fog. The Kingdom is not distant; it is near. It begins the moment truth replaces pride.

"Therefore if any man be in Christ, he is a new creature: old things are passed away; behold, all things are become new."

—2 Corinthians 5:17

The "new earth" begins not in geography but in the heart. Every soul awakened by the Spirit is already walking its unseen soil. When you live by truth, forgive freely, and love without reward, you are already breathing the air of the world to come.

"For, behold, the kingdom of God is within you."—Luke 17:21

This is the mystery Revelation unveils—not merely the end of an age, but the unveiling of what has been here all along: the true world breaking through the false, heaven quietly reclaiming earth through willing hearts.

The Kingdom is already alive, though not yet complete. Creation still groans, but its renewal has begun. Every act of faith, every word of truth, every quiet kindness is a seed of what will one day cover the earth.

You are not escaping the world—you are glimpsing its restoration. You are walking the edge of the New Earth before it is fully revealed.

"Behold, I make all things new."—*Revelation 21:5*

Appendix A

God's Revealed Truths

Foundations that do not move.

1. God Is the Creator of All Things

"In the beginning, God created the heaven and the earth." (Genesis 1:1)

"For by him were all things created, that are in heaven, and that are in earth." (Colossians 1:16)

2. God Made Humanity in His Image

"So God created man in His own image." (Genesis 1:27)
"Thou hast formed me in my mother's womb." (cf. Psalm 139:13)

3. God Created Two Sexes—Male and Female

"Male and female created He them." (Genesis 1:27)
"But from the beginning creation God made them male and female." (Mark 10:6)

4. God Is Holy, Righteous, and Just

"Holy, holy, holy is the Lord of hosts." (Isaiah 6:3)
"The Lord is righteous in all His ways, and holy in all His works" (Psalm 145:17)

5. Sin Is Real and Separates Us from God

"For all have sinned and come short of the glory of God." (Romans 3:23)

"The wages of sin is death." (Romans 6:23)

6. Jesus Christ Alone Is Lord and Savior

"I am the way, the truth, and the life." (John 14:6)

"For God so loved the world that He gave His only begotten Son" (John 3:16)

7. Salvation Is a Gift—Received by Grace Through Faith

"That if thou shalt confess with thy mouth the Lord Jesus, and shalt believe in thine heart that God hath raised him from the dead, thou shalt be saved." (Romans 10:9)

8. The Holy Spirit Dwells in God's People

"But the Comforter, which is the Holy Ghost, whom the Father will send in my name, he shall teach you all things, and bring all things to your remembrance, whatsoever I have said unto you." (John 14:26)

9. God's Word Is Truth

"Thy word is a lamp unto my feet and a light unto my path." (Psalm 119:105)

"Sanctify them through thy truth; thy word is truth." (John 17:17)

10. God Designed Marriage, Family, and Covenant Love

"A man shall leave his father and mother and shall cleave unto his wife." (Genesis 2:24)

"Children are a heritage of the Lord." (Psalm 127:3)

11. Christ Will Return and Judge the Living and the Dead

"For we must all appear before the judgment seat of Christ." (2 Corinthians 5:10)

"Behold, He cometh with clouds, and every eye shall see Him." (Revelation 1:7)

12. Eternal Life Awaits Those Who Belong to Him

"God shall wipe away all tears… and there shall be no more death." (Revelation 21:4) "And so shall we ever be with the Lord." (1 Thessalonians 4:17)

13. Life Is Sacred

From conception to Eternity

"Before I formed thee in the belly I knew thee." (Jeremiah 1:5) "In Him we live and move and have our being." (Acts 17:28) Human life carries the image of God. It is not defined by man's approval but by God's creation.

These are not opinions. These are foundations.

The world shifts—the Word does not.

Appendix B

A Biblical Blueprint for Life & Salvation

How to walk with God in a world that forgets Him.

1. Love God First

"Thou shalt love the Lord thy God with all thy heart, and with all thy soul, and with all thy mind."(Matthew 22:37)
Every virtue flows from this. Place God first in prayer, Scripture, worship, and daily decisions.

2. Care for Body & Spirit

"He giveth His beloved sleep" (Psalm 127:2).
Eat well, move often—avoid habits that dull the soul (cf. Proverbs 23:20–21).

3. Honor Family—Begin at Home

"Provide for your own… especially for those of your own house." (1 Timothy 5:8)
"Honour thy father and thy mother" (Exodus 20:12)
"And, ye fathers, provoke not your children to wrath: but bring them up in the nurture and admonition of the Lord." (Ephesians 6:4)

4. Work Diligently & Honestly

"Do it heartily as to the Lord" (Colossians 3:23)."Wealth gotten by vanity shall be diminished: but he that gathereth by labour shall increase."(Proverbs 13:11)

5. Walk in Humility & Modesty

"God… giveth grace unto the humble."(James 4:6).
"Let another man praise thee, and not thine own mouth." (Proverbs 27:2)

6. Marriage & Family as God Designed

"Husbands, love your wives…" (Ephesians 5:25)

Marriage is built on sacrificial love and shared honor.

A husband protects and serves; a wife strengthens with grace.

Children are gift, joy, legacy—not burden. The home is where love is learned and lived.

7. Choose Friends and Community Wisely

"He that walketh with wise men shall be wise…" (Proverbs 13:20)

Choose companions who sharpen virtue, not dull it.

Give freely and gladly — generosity multiplies joy.

Forgive without delay; grace restores what bitterness breaks.

A good life is built through wisdom, open hands, and a soft heart.

8. Guard Heart, Mind, and Tongue

"Death and life are in the power of the tongue…" (Proverbs 18:21)Speak carefully — words cut or heal.

Restrain anger; a quiet spirit holds strength.

Fill the mind with what is pure, noble, and good.

The heart is shaped by what we say, dwell on, and allow to rule us.

9. Grow Spiritually Every Day

"Pray without ceasing" (1 Thessalonians 5:17).

Growth is not rushed; it is rooted. Day by day, the soul becomes strong.

10. Live with Eternity in View

"Seek ye first the kingdom of God…"(Matthew 6:33).

Christ will return, and every soul will stand before Him.

Live now for what outlasts the world.

11. Steward Money with Wisdom

"Honour the Lord with thy substance."(Proverbs 3:9).

Money is a tool, not a master.

Its love corrupts, but its wise use blesses.

Work diligently, save patiently, give freely—and live content.
Wealth is temporary; integrity is treasure.

12. Speak Truth with Love

Let no corrupt communication proceed out of your mouth (Ephesians 4:29).

Truth delivered in love builds homes, hearts, and hope. What we say becomes what others carry. Let it be life.

13. Time Is a Stewardship

"So teach us to number our days, that we may apply our hearts unto wisdom." (Psalm 90:12)

Seek God first each day, work well, and rest without guilt. Use hours wisely, knowing they do not return.

14. Salvation Begins with Knowing God

I am the way ,the truth, and the life (John 14:6).

We were made for God — to know Him, walk with Him, and reflect His likeness. Sin shattered that fellowship, leaving every soul short of glory. But Christ restores what was broken. Through His death and resurrection, we are invited home again — forgiven, renewed, alive.

15. Salvation Produces New Birth

"Therefore if any man be in Christ, he is a new creature: old things are passed away; behold, all things are become new." (2 Corinthians 5:17)

Turn from sin and walk as His disciple.

16. Live Daily by the Spirit

"Exhort one another daily… lest any of you be hardened through the deceitfulness of sin." (Hebrews 3:13)

Obey God with a willing heart.

17. Serve with Purpose

"And whatsoever ye do, do it heartily, as to the Lord, and not unto men." (Colossians 3:23)

Let your life become ministry.

18. Persevere Through Trials

"Being confident of this very thing, that he which hath begun a good work in you will perform it until the day of Jesus Christ." (Philippians 1:6)

Stand—even when the world falls.

19. Our Hope Is Eternal Life

"God shall wipe away all tears… and there shall be no more death, neither sorrow, nor crying, neither shall there be any more pain." (Revelation 21:4)

The blueprint ends in glory.

Fix your eyes on Christ—and walk toward the Kingdom.

Appendix C

Sins & Temptations That Lead the Soul Away

The pitfalls Scripture reveals.

1. Idolatry & False Worship

When anything becomes more important than God, even good things become gods.

"Thou shalt have no other gods before Me." (Exodus 20:3)

2. Sexual Immorality

"The works of the flesh are manifest, which are these; Adultery, fornication, uncleanness, lasciviousness…" (Galatians 5:19)

God designed sexual intimacy to flourish within marriage— one man, one woman, one covenant. Anything outside that— no matter how culture renames it—leads to harm. Boundaries don't restrict love. They protect it.

3. Pride & Arrogance

Pride is the seed of every rebellion—Satan fell by it, nations collapse under it.

"Pride goes before destruction." (Proverbs 16:18)

"God opposes the proud but gives grace to the humble." (James 4:6)

4. Greed & Love of Money

Money is a tool—but worship it, and it becomes a master.

"For the love of money is the root of all of evil." (1 Timothy 6:10)

"A man's life consisteth not in the things he possesseth."(Luke 12:15)

5. Anger, Hatred & Unforgiveness

Bitterness poisons the soul more than the offender—forgiveness frees.

"But I say unto you, That whosoever is angry with his brother without a cause shall be in danger of the judgment…" (Matthew 5:22)

6. Drunkenness & Gluttony

Anything that numbs the Spirit—food, drink, or pleasure—becomes a trap.

"Drunkenness… they which do such things shall not inherit the kingdom of God." (Galatians 5:21)

7. Lying, Gossip & Corrupt Speech

Tongues can kill with quieter blades than swords—God calls words to truth.

"The Lord hates a lying tongue, and he that soweth discord among brethren." (Proverbs 6:16–19)

8. Envy, Jealousy & Coveting

Comparison steals joy, poisons gratitude, and blinds us to our own calling.

"For where envying and strife is, there is confusion and every evil work."(James 3:16)

"Thou shalt not covet." (Exodus 20:17)

9. Laziness & Neglect of Duty

God honors diligence—apathy wastes the gifts He gives.

"The soul of the sluggard desireth, and hath nothing: but the soul of the diligent shall be made fat."(Proverbs 13:4)

"If anyone would not work, neither should he eat."

(2 Thessalonians 3:10)

10. Unbelief & Rejecting Truth

Judgment begins not with sin, but with refusing the remedy.

"Take heed… lest there be in you an evil heart of unbelief, in departing from the living God." (Hebrews 3:12)

"God shall send them strong delusion, that they should believe a lie." (2 Thessalonians 2:11–12)

Appendix D

Grace & Forgiveness

The gates of mercy are never closed.

1. Forgiveness Is Always Available

No matter the stain, the door swings open to the one who turns back.

2. No Sin Lies Beyond Redemption

God does not just erase guilt—He transforms the guilty into witnesses.

3. Christ Took Our Place

Forgiveness is not cheap—it was purchased by blood and offered freely.

4. Repentance Leads to New Life

Repentance is not shame—it is rebirth, a doorway into joy.

5. No Condemnation for Those in Christ

Grace does more than forgive—it removes the voice of accusation forever.

Appendix E

Discernment & Judgment

We do not judge to condemn—we judge to guard what God has entrusted.

Scripture does not forbid judgment—it forbids proud judgment. Christ commands not blindness, but clarity. Not accusation, but discernment. We are called to evaluate teachings, character, and influence—with humility, patience, and the fruit of the Spirit.

1. What Jesus Taught

Jesus warned against shallow judgment, yet He commanded wise judgment.

We do not condemn souls—that is God's throne alone.
But we do weigh fruit, influence, tone, and pattern.

"Judge not according to the appearance, but judger righteous judgment." (John 7:24)

"Ye shall know them by their fruits." (Matthew 7:16)

"He that is spiritual judgeth all things…" (1 Corinthians 2:15)

"Prove all things; hold fast that which is good."
(1 Thessalonians 5:21)

2. Fruit Reveals the Root

The surest test of a life is what grows from it.
Love • Joy • Peace • Patience • Kindness • Goodness
Faithfulness • Gentleness • Self-control
Where these grow, Christ is near.

Immorality • Hatred • Jealousy • Fits of rage • Selfish
ambition • Division • Envy • Drunkenness • Wild indulgence
Where these dominate, something else is ruling.
No mask can hide fruit forever.

3. Other Biblical Litmus Tests

Pure • Peace-loving • Gentle • Merciful • Impartial • Sincere
If it divides, flatters, or stirs chaos—it is not wisdom from
God.
Wolves wear wool—only time unmasks them.
Teachings must be tested, not trusted by default.
If love is absent, even miracles mean nothing.
Discernment always asks: *Does this reflect Christ?*

4. The Balance of Judgment

True discernment is humility with clarity.
We evaluate—we do not exalt ourselves as judge.
You may judge conduct, but not eternal fate.
Watch for fruit, not flare.
Talent is not righteousness—outcome reveals truth.
Pray for wisdom.
Discernment protects the home, guides the heart, and
preserves the soul.

5. On Instinct, and the Deception of "Good Fruits"

Not every appearance of goodness is good.
Predators, false teachers, manipulators, and those who seek
advantage can imitate virtue for a short season. They borrow
the language of kindness, cloak themselves in a moment of
humility, or mimic the outward fruits of the Spirit long
enough to persuade the undiscerning.
But imitation cannot endure.
Counterfeit fruit rots quickly.
Discernment includes the courage to trust the quiet alarms
within—the instincts, intuition, and inner warnings that the
Spirit often uses to protect us. Not all hesitation is fear.
Sometimes it is wisdom.

As Christ warned:

"Beware of false prophets, which come to you in sheep's clothing, but inwardly they are ravening wolves."

(Matthew 7:15)

True fruit remains.

False fruit collapses under time, pressure, or truth.

To walk in discernment is to listen when the spirit within speaks, *"Something is off."* It is not suspicion—it is stewardship of your life, your peace, and those entrusted to you.

6. Guarding Your Own House and City Before Aiding Others

Discernment also means knowing the order of responsibility. A house must be strengthened before it can shelter others. A city must be guarded before it can send help to its neighbors. Stability is not selfish—it is the necessary ground from which generosity can flourish.

You do not bring wolves into your fold.

You do not import chaos in the name of compassion.

You go to help it, but you do not let it overrun your gates.

This is the ancient pattern of wisdom:

"Every wise woman buildeth her house:

but the foolish plucketh it down with her hands."

(Proverbs 14:1)

Strength first, then service.

Order first, then outreach.

A fortified house can rescue the weak.

A guarded city can extend mercy without being conquered by the very troubles it seeks to heal.

In every generation, discernment means protecting what is good, preserving what is entrusted, and carrying light outward—not dragging darkness inward.

7. Boundaries Are Not Fear—They Are Stewardship

In every age, the collapse of boundaries has been mistaken for the rise of virtue. But in Scripture, boundaries are not signs of fear—they are signs of wisdom.

A garden without a wall is not generous; it is vulnerable.

A city without gates is not welcoming; it is defenseless.

A home without discernment is not loving; it is exposed.

Compassion without structure becomes chaos.

Generosity without order becomes exploitation.

Mercy without judgment becomes permission for harm.

Boundaries are there to guard what God has entrusted to you — your home, your community, your peace—so that they remain strong enough to bless others.

Boundaries are not barriers against love;

they are the frameworks that make love sustainable.

As Proverbs teaches:

"Keep thy heart with all diligence;

for out of it are the issues of life." (Proverbs 4:23)

To foresee danger is not cowardice.

It is stewardship—the mature recognition that what is nurtured and protected can grow, flourish, and extend help outward in strength rather than collapse inward from harm. Boundaries do not contradict compassion. They enable it. Judgment protects the family, and preserves truth in a deceptive age. Christ gave us a standard clear enough to follow and humble enough to soften:

Not by charm.

Not by charisma.

By fruit.

That is biblical judgment—humble, watchful, grounded.

8. Truth Is Not Personal—It Is Found

The modern world has embraced a belief that sounds compassionate but is spiritually disastrous:

"Everyone has their own truth."

This single idea has unraveled discernment more than nearly anything else in our time.

Here is why.

I. If truth is personal, then no warning is valid.

You cannot caution someone if danger itself is "subjective."
The watchman's trumpet is silenced by accusation:
"That's just your perspective."
But Scripture gives truth the authority to warn, redirect, and
protect.

II. Personal truth erases objective boundaries.

When truth becomes internal:
No behavior may be judged
No ideology may be tested
No motive may be questioned
No fruit may be examined
Through relativism, deception becomes invisible.

III. Harm cannot be named if every action is "someone's truth."

If morality is self-defined, then:
Predators become "misunderstood"
Manipulators become "expressing themselves"
Evil becomes "a different viewpoint"
Without objective truth, society loses the ability to identify
wolves at all.

IV. Self-sacrifice becomes performance instead of wisdom.

When "openness" becomes the only virtue, people feel pressured to:

Remove boundaries

Invite chaos

Deny danger

Accept harm as moral proof

This is not compassion.

It is theater that destroys the very home from which compassion should flow.

V. Instinct and discernment are shamed into silence.

People are told:

"If something feels wrong, it's your prejudice, not the danger."

God-given intuition—a primary tool of discernment—is treated as a flaw rather than a protection.

This leaves individuals and communities exposed.

VI. The foundation collapses because truth is no longer a Person, but a preference.

Christ did not say:

"I am *a* truth."

He said:

"I am the way, the truth, and the life."

Subjective truth erases the need for discernment, judgment, and watchfulness—because if everyone is right, no one can be warned. Scripture restores the foundation:

"Sanctify them through thy truth: thy word is truth."

(John 17:17)

Truth is not crafted. Truth is revealed.

Truth is not internal. Truth is eternal.

To return to discernment, we must return to *The Truth*—objective, unchanging, God-given. Only then can boundaries be rebuilt, instincts honored, and wisdom restored.

Appendix F

The Dignity & Sanctity of Human Life

Life is sacred because it comes from God.
We do not define its worth—we recognize it.

Every human life carries the image of God—the unborn, the elderly, the healthy, the broken, the strong, the weak.
The value of a life does not come from ability, utility, age, or approval—it comes from *Imago Dei*.

Life is not sacred because it is beautiful.
It is sacred because it is His.

1. Life Begins With God

"A man can receive nothing, except it be given him from heaven."(John 3:27)
Life is not an accident of biology—it is a gift of breath from eternity.

2. The Unborn Belong to Him

"Before I formed thee… I sanctified thee." (Jeremiah 1:5)
God knows life before it is visible. Not potential life—present life, hidden life.

3. The Weak Are Not Less Valuable

"As ye have done it unto the least of these… ye have done it unto me."(Matthew 25:40)

God's image does not fade with illness, disability, or age.

4. We Honor God by Honoring Life

"Deliver them that are drawn unto death." (Proverbs 24:11)

Protecting life is worship. To defend the vulnerable is obedience.

5. Life is Eternal in Christ

"This is life eternal, that they might know thee."(John 17:3)

Earthly life is precious—but it is *prelude*, not conclusion.

Final Thought

Human dignity is not fragile—it is eternal.

Because life belongs to God, love is its law, and Christ is its worth.

Thank you for reading.

For more information about upcoming volumes in The Word Thru Time or other works by the author, please visit: www.CyborgHunter.com

If you'd like to reach out, you can email: cyborghunter@cyborghunter.com

www.ingramcontent.com/pod-product-compliance
Lightning Source LLC
Chambersburg PA
CBHW021206130626
46554CB00005B/2009